I0408007

IRAN ON NOTICE

HEARING

BEFORE THE

COMMITTEE ON FOREIGN AFFAIRS
HOUSE OF REPRESENTATIVES

ONE HUNDRED FIFTEENTH CONGRESS

FIRST SESSION

FEBRUARY 16, 2017

Serial No. 115–5

Printed for the use of the Committee on Foreign Affairs

Available via the World Wide Web: http://www.foreignaffairs.house.gov/ or
http://www.gpo.gov/fdsys/

U.S. GOVERNMENT PUBLISHING OFFICE

24–242PDF   WASHINGTON : 2017

For sale by the Superintendent of Documents, U.S. Government Publishing Office
Internet: bookstore.gpo.gov   Phone: toll free (866) 512–1800; DC area (202) 512–1800
Fax: (202) 512–2104   Mail: Stop IDCC, Washington, DC 20402–0001

COMMITTEE ON FOREIGN AFFAIRS

EDWARD R. ROYCE, California, *Chairman*

CHRISTOPHER H. SMITH, New Jersey
ILEANA ROS-LEHTINEN, Florida
DANA ROHRABACHER, California
STEVE CHABOT, Ohio
JOE WILSON, South Carolina
MICHAEL T. McCAUL, Texas
TED POE, Texas
DARRELL E. ISSA, California
TOM MARINO, Pennsylvania
JEFF DUNCAN, South Carolina
MO BROOKS, Alabama
PAUL COOK, California
SCOTT PERRY, Pennsylvania
RON DeSANTIS, Florida
MARK MEADOWS, North Carolina
TED S. YOHO, Florida
ADAM KINZINGER, Illinois
LEE M. ZELDIN, New York
DANIEL M. DONOVAN, JR., New York
F. JAMES SENSENBRENNER, JR.,
  Wisconsin
ANN WAGNER, Missouri
BRIAN J. MAST, Florida
FRANCIS ROONEY, Florida
BRIAN K. FITZPATRICK, Pennsylvania
THOMAS A. GARRETT, JR., Virginia

ELIOT L. ENGEL, New York
BRAD SHERMAN, California
GREGORY W. MEEKS, New York
ALBIO SIRES, New Jersey
GERALD E. CONNOLLY, Virginia
THEODORE E. DEUTCH, Florida
KAREN BASS, California
WILLIAM R. KEATING, Massachusetts
DAVID N. CICILLINE, Rhode Island
AMI BERA, California
LOIS FRANKEL, Florida
TULSI GABBARD, Hawaii
JOAQUIN CASTRO, Texas
ROBIN L. KELLY, Illinois
BRENDAN F. BOYLE, Pennsylvania
DINA TITUS, Nevada
NORMA J. TORRES, California
BRADLEY SCOTT SCHNEIDER, Illinois
THOMAS R. SUOZZI, New York
ADRIANO ESPAILLAT, New York
TED LIEU, California

AMY PORTER, *Chief of Staff*   THOMAS SHEEHY, *Staff Director*
JASON STEINBAUM, *Democratic Staff Director*

CONTENTS

IRAN ON NOTICE

THURSDAY, FEBRUARY 16, 2017

House of Representatives,
Committee on Foreign Affairs,
Washington, DC.

The committee met, pursuant to notice, at 10:00 a.m., in room 2172 Rayburn House Office Building, Hon. Edward Royce (chairman of the committee) presiding.

Chairman ROYCE. This hearing will come to order. This morning we consider options available to the new administration as it contends with an emboldened Iran.

As one witness will tell the committee, we should start with this premise: Iran "gets no special pass" on its dangerous and provocative acts. Unfortunately—despite its promises to the committee—that is not how the previous administration handled Tehran. Terrorist and missile activities that should have been designated were not designated. In a country where beatings and torture and executions are the norm, just one individual has been sanctioned for human rights abuses after negotiations began, just one. After that deal was inked, the former Secretary of State traveled the world enthusiastically touting that Iran was open for business.

Indeed, the administration went out of its way not to offend Tehran. In December, when this committee pressed the extension of the Iran Sanctions Act, the President took the very unusual step of letting this legislation become law without his signature.

So it is not surprising that Tehran believes it is in a "post-sanctions environment." But as long as Iran is firing missiles, fueling terror, and shouting "Death to America," nothing can be normal.

Sanctions can be imposed even while adhering to and strictly enforcing the nuclear agreement—as flawed as it is. Remember, even under the previous administration's reading, the administration has the ability to press back on Iran's support for terrorism, for human rights abuses, and for missile development. "None of these sanctions were relieved under the [agreement]," in the words of the former administration.

So Iran's continuing intercontinental ballistic missile program—whose only purpose is to carry a nuclear warhead—must be front and center. This month's designations are a good start. But more can be done to find and target the banks and companies that are supplying this dangerous program aimed at us. It also means more extraditions, more prosecutions, and indictments of sanctions violators. This proactive approach also means stepping up our defenses and those of our regional partners.

(1)

Second, the administration shouldn't be shy about tackling Iran's terror arm and that is the Islamic Revolutionary Guard Corps. This is the group fueling the Assad regime in Syria and this is the group responsible for the death of hundreds of American troops. Since the Guard has been labeled Iran's "most powerful economic actor" by the U.S. Treasury Department, there are plenty of options here available. Indeed, there are hundreds of Iranian Revolutionary Guard Corps affiliates that are yet to be sanctioned—what one ob-server calls a "Revolutionary Guard's Gap." These are the front companies that are funding the missiles that have on the side of them, "Israel must be wiped off the face of the earth."

These terror outfits need to be sanctioned, and the new adminis-tration should look at ways in which companies closely linked to the Revolutionary Guard Corps—but not fully owned by them—could be sanctioned. The threat of secondary sanctions against those around the world dealing with these IRGC units which even tried to carry out a terrorist attack here in Washington, DC, to kill the Saudi Ambassador here in Washington. Looking at this must be a priority, and it has to be real, and it wasn't under the previous administration.

Around the region, the administration can attack Iran's proxy Hezbollah thanks to a new law advanced by this committee. We can focus on increased interdiction of Iranian arms shipments to the revolutionary Houthis in Yemen, on clearer rules of engage-ment, and better defense cooperation with our partners on the front lines of the Iranian threat.

The nuclear agreement does not leave us defenseless against Tehran's threatening behavior. Careful coordination with allies is a must, and all along we should be clear that the choice is with Iran to end its threatening, destabilizing behavior.

I am going to introduce our panel this morning, and then I am going to go to Mr. Eliot Engel of New York who is the ranking member of this committee.

On our panel we have Ms. Katherine Bauer. She is the Blumenstein-Katz Family Fellow at The Washington Institute for Near East Policy and previously she served in a series of positions at the Treasury Department.

We have Mr. David Albright. He is the founder and president of the Institute for Science and International Security. Mr. Albright is a trained physicist and former weapons inspector.

We have Mr. Scott Modell, managing director at the Rapidan Group and previously served for 13 years in the Central Intel-ligence Agency.

And we have Dr. Andrew Exum, contributing editor at the Atlan-tic and previously Dr. Exum served as Deputy Assistant Secretary of Defense for Middle East Policy.

Without objection, the witnesses' full prepared statements are going to be made part of the record and you will be asked to sum-marize if you could. The members here are going to have 5 cal-endar days to submit any statements or additional questions, any extraneous material they might want to put into the record.

So we would start with Ms. Bauer, but before we do that allow me to have the ranking member of the committee Eliot Engel open with his opening comments.

Mr. ENGEL. Well, thank you. Thank you very much, Mr. Chairman, and let me also thank our witnesses and welcome all of you to the Foreign Affairs Committee.

At this point we all know Iran's record of provocative actions, from ballistic missile tests to transferring weapons to terrorist organizations and other bad actors that seek to destabilize the region. Technically speaking, all this bad behavior doesn't violate the nuclear deal. However, those actions are inconsistent with U.N. Security Council Resolution 2231 which governs the implementation of the agreement. Responsible governments around the world have an obligation to respond.

The Trump administration imposed new sanctions against several entities involved in Iran's ballistic missile program and support for terrorism. And just to make sure we are all being fair, I will mention that these designations matched exactly the Obama administration's response over the last several years since negotiations began.

The difference between the Trump administration's response and the Obama administration's response was a two-word phrase, "on notice." Then National Security Advisor Mike Flynn said as a result of Iran's provocative actions the United States is putting Iran "on notice." So what does it mean exactly to put Iran "on notice"? How will the administration respond if Iran tests the President again? Does the administration have a plan?

In a follow-up briefing to the "on notice" warning a reporter asked what that meant. The response was, "We are considering what options there are and how we want to communicate and enforce our concerns." That is not really a plan. I hope that the administration will make it clear what their plan is on Iran because surely Iran will continue its provocative behavior.

We cannot afford a half-baked or reckless foreign policy. Rash decisions concerning America's role in the world could have serious consequences for American personnel and interests. American and Iranian forces are operating in close proximity in Iraq. Who knows what could happen if the administration doesn't have a cohesive policy? Additionally, if this turns out to be an empty threat, then this administration will not have done its job. We have to really confront the Iranian threat and let them know that we are serious about it, that we mean business.

I don't trust the Iranian Government. I didn't vote for the Iranian deal. But the Iranian deal is now in place and I think we have to ensure that Iran lives up to every bit of its responsibility under that deal. Let me just say this. I look forward to our hearing from our witnesses about what a responsible course of action would be. Iran and the terrible regime in Tehran is not going away and I think that if the United States doesn't stand up to it, it will only get worse. I believe with all my heart that everything must be done to prevent Iran from having a nuclear weapon. However, looking the other way and just tough rhetoric doesn't really cut the mustard. We have got to make sure that Iran understands that there are severe consequences if they continue their ways. And I look forward to hearing from our witnesses as to what they think our response should be.

Thank you, Mr. Chairman.

Chairman ROYCE. Thank you very much, Mr. Engel. We now go to our witnesses.

Ms. Bauer.

STATEMENT OF MS. KATHERINE BAUER, BLUMENSTEIN-KATZ FAMILY FELLOW, THE WASHINGTON INSTITUTE FOR NEAR EAST POLICY

Ms. BAUER. Good morning. Chairman Royce, Ranking Member Engel and members of the committee. Thank you for the opportunity to testify before you today to discuss the future of U.S. policy toward Iran. My testimony will focus on the role of sanctions and restraining Iran's malign influence in the region and disrupting its global terrorism, money laundering, and procurement networks. It will draw on analysis done in conjunction with my colleagues Patrick Clawson and Matthew Levitt at the Washington Institute for Near East Policy as part of a new study that we released earlier this week. I will summarize key points here.

There is no doubt today that sanctions played a pivotal role in bringing Iran to the table to negotiate constraints on its nuclear program. Over roughly a decade, the U.S. and its allies imposed powerful multilateral sanctions on Iran that isolated Tehran from the international financial system and crippled its economy.

Following implementation of the Iran nuclear deal in January 2016 and suspension of nuclear related sanctions, the pace of sanctions against Iran under remaining authorities slowed. Despite assurances the United States would vigorously press against Iranian activities outside of the Joint Comprehensive Plan of Action, the Obama administration did so only sporadically. Thus, in many ways Washington ceded the narrative to Tehran which successfully convinced many in the private and public sectors that in the wake of implementation of the nuclear agreement they operate in a post sanctions environment.

But the deal was never intended to give Iran a free pass on its nonnuclear malevolent actions. Iran made no commitment to cease nonnuclear malign activity and has not in fact halted it. In the words of Abbas Araqchi, Iran's deputy foreign minister and one of Iran's chief negotiators of the deal, "During the nuclear negotiations we clearly said that questions of security, defense, ballistic missiles and our regional policies were not negotiable and not linked to the nuclear talks."

Sanctions remain a viable and powerful tool to confront Iran over its nonnuclear illicit conduct. In our study we suggest a multipronged approach that includes taking back the narrative, emphasizing the sanctions that remain, and vigorously enforcing them. Such enhanced sanctions will work best, however, if they are proportional and accompanied by diplomatic, military, and intelligence measures in a coordinated campaign against Iran's destabilizing activities.

Sanctions are a tool in such a strategy, but not a strategy unto themselves. There is a place for unilateral sanctions such as the action taken by the Trump administration late last month against Iranian procurement and terrorist support networks. These actions were likely prepared under the Obama administration, and as Congressman Engel noted they demonstrate a bipartisan consensus on targeting Iran's malign activities. They are also effective because banks around the world look to the U.S. and to the OFAC list and they can be very disruptive. As well, they lay the groundwork for other countries to follow suit.

However, sanctions are most effective when adopted by an international coalition. Foreign partners have long been skeptical of U.S. unilateral sanctions when they are viewed as being capricious. Thus, focusing on Iranian conduct that violates international norms will be most likely to draw multilateral support and compliance. In this manner, sanctions can also demonstrate to Iran the benefits of accommodating itself to the international order.

Consider the benefits that Iran has gleaned from the nuclear deal. Oil sales and other exports are up and inflation has stabilized. Iranian officials claim that hundreds of small banks have already reestablished correspondent relationships with Iran. But Iran will not be able to attract the foreign investment it desperately needs while global banks continue to view it as a financial pariah, and there is no reason to believe that Iran has ceased the illicit financial conduct or sanctions evasion conduct that underpinned the U.S. FinCEN 311 finding of Iran as a jurisdiction of Primary Money Laundering Concern or earned Iran its place on the Financial Action Task Force blacklist.

Previously, private sector engagement on the risks of doing business with Iran proved incredibly effective as a tool to restrict Iran's operating environment. Given this history, the U.S. Government should resume such sanctions diplomacy and engagements with private and public sector actors around the world to highlight evidence that Iran continues to pose a threat to the global financial system. Rather than reassuring banks that doing business with Iran will help enshrine the nuclear deal, U.S. Government officials at every level should emphasize that Iran bears the onus of demonstrating its adherence to the same requirements imposed on every other country by reining in illicit financial activity and conforming with international norms.

Thank you again for the opportunity to testify.

[The prepared statement of Ms. Bauer follows:]

Iran on Notice

Katherine Bauer
Blumenstein-Katz Family Fellow,
The Washington Institute for Near East Policy

Testimony submitted to the House Committee on Foreign Affairs
February 16, 2017

Chairman Royce, Ranking Member Engel, and members of the committee, thank you for the opportunity to appear before you to discuss the future of U.S. policy toward Iran. My testimony will focus on the role of sanctions in restraining Iran's malign influence in the region and disrupting its global-terrorism, money-laundering and procurement networks. Much of the following comes from analysis done in conjunction with my colleagues Patrick Clawson and Matthew Levitt at the Washington Institute for Near East Policy as part of a new study released earlier this week.[1]

INTRODUCTION

Following implementation of the Iran nuclear deal in January 2016, and suspension of nuclear-related sanctions, the pace of new Iran-related designations under remaining authorities slowed. Despite assurances that that United States would "vigorously press sanctions against Iranian activities outside of the Joint Comprehensive Plan of Action," [2] the Obama administration did so only sporadically. Thus, in many ways, Washington ceded the narrative to Tehran, which successfully convinced many in the private and public sectors that in the wake of implementation of the nuclear agreement, they operate in a "post-sanctions environment."

However, sanctions remain a viable and powerful tool for Congress and the new administration to confront Iran over human rights abuses, terror support, and ballistic missile tests. In our study, we suggest that the new administration adopt a multipronged approach to reinforcing the role of sanctions in restraining Iranian aggression in the region and other malign activities. This approach involves taking back the narrative about the deal by emphasizing the sanctions that remain; fully implementing those sanctions; imposing additional sanctions for nonnuclear transgressions; and applying proportional sanctions when Iran fails to comply with part of the nuclear deal.

Enhanced sanctions will work best if they are accompanied by diplomatic, military, and intelligence measures in a coordinated campaign against Iran's destabilizing activities. Likewise, sanctions are most effective when they are adopted by an international coalition. Foreign partners have long been skeptical of U.S. unilateral sanctions when they are viewed as being capricious. Focusing on Iranian conduct that violates international norms will thus be most likely to draw multilateral support. Relatedly, demonstrating international resolve on nonnuclear issues is more apt to garner Iranian respect for the constraints of the deal itself.

EMPHASIZE REMAINING SANCTIONS

The first component of this multipronged strategy is to change the narrative holding that sanctions are going away: this is not a post-sanctions environment, and Iran's ongoing illicit conduct is the reason for continued sanctions. Indeed, Iran made no commitment to cease nonnuclear malign activity and has not, in fact, halted it. In the words of Abbas Araqchi, Iran's deputy foreign minister and one of Iran's chief negotiators of the deal, "During the nuclear negotiations, we clearly said that questions of security, defense, ballistic missile and our regional policies were not negotiable and not linked to the nuclear talks."[3] In fact, according to the top U.S. military commander in the Middle East, Army Gen. Joseph Votel, Iran has been more aggressive regionally since implementation of the nuclear agreement.[4] Yet Iran is in complete control on this front: it can alter its behavior and cease engaging in illicit conduct, in which case sanctions will be removed. For the United States, rather than talking about reimposing suspended sanctions, which would receive strong pushback from U.S. allies, the narrative should be about exposing and disrupting persons and entities on still-sanctionable grounds.

Part of this new narrative involves repeating the statement that Iran remains subject to international norms. The idea is simple: "Iran gets no special pass." The nuclear accord does not prevent the imposition of nonnuclear sanctions or the use of other tools to contest such illicit conduct, just as arms treaties with the former Soviet Union did not spare it from other sanctions. Such an effort will be aimed, as noted, at changing the perception that sanctions are going away and the related Iranian narrative that any remaining restrictions signal bad faith by the United States.

Public statements should focus on the behavior that elicits sanctions, not the chilling impact they could have on investment in Iran or the uncertainty new sanctions would introduce. That said, the Trump administration should counter claims that the sanctions relief was "front-loaded" and make clear that a snapback of sanctions would have profound consequences for Iran. In doing so, Washington should emphasize that Iran still has much to lose—the bulk of Iran's no-longer-restricted assets remain offshore—and that renewed financial and commercial relationships remain tenuous. Statements should make a strong, direct case that Iran is violating international norms when it engages in deceptive behavior to deliver support to terrorist organizations; clandestine procurement for its missile program; use of information technology to suppress human rights; or violations of UN Security Council arms embargoes. The new U.S. administration should also make plain that the United States will expose and disrupt Iran's use of proxies to create plausible deniability and threaten asymmetric retaliation. The credibility of financial sanctions, and the ability to leverage them to build a multinational coalition, depends on responding directly to Iranian behavior and not casting sanctions-related actions as a tool of economic warfare.

Since the aim is to rally international support by showing that Iran rather than the United States is breaking the rules, sanctions enforcement should not be explained as a tactic to toughen the nuclear deal. Indeed, implying that the sanctions are meant to create uncertainty in the marketplace—to prevent Iran from benefiting from its yield from the nuclear deal—reinforces Iran's narrative that the United

States isn't living up to its commitments under the Joint Comprehensive Plan of Action (JCPOA), as the deal is known. Likewise, revising or rescinding technical guidance on sanctions relief risks delegitimizing the Office of Foreign Assets Control (OFAC) in its role as technical implementer of sanctions policy. After all, the guidance is a reflection of underlying statute and regulation and does not alter legal realities. Furthermore, many of the regulatory realities reflect positions taken across U.S. sanctions programs and are not specific to the Iran program. Across-the-board changes may have unintended consequences on other sanctions programs, whereas changing the rules only for Iran would complicate implementation.

Private-sector engagement on the risks of doing business with Iran opened up political space for European and Asian states to join in U.S.-led efforts to impose nuclear-related sanctions on the Islamic Republic. Given this history, the U.S. government should resume engagements with private- and public-sector actors around the world to highlight evidence that Iran continues to pose a threat to the global financial system. Rather than reassuring banks that doing business with Iran can help enshrine the nuclear deal, U.S. government officials at every level should emphasize that Iran bears the onus of demonstrating its adherence to the same requirements imposed on every other country by reining in illicit financial activity and conforming with international norms for its financial system. U.S. officials should also highlight the continued UN Security Council restrictions that Iran violates, including the embargo on Iranian arms exports extended under Security Council Resolution 2231 and the UN embargo on arming Hezbollah in Syria and the Houthis in Yemen. Recall that a number of Iranian individuals and entities sanctioned under earlier Security Council resolutions for their role in WMD procurement and weapons exports remain on the UN list. Also to be emphasized is that regional bodies concur with the United States that Hezbollah is a terrorist group—both the European Union and the Gulf Cooperation Council have designated Hezbollah in part or in full—and that Iranian human rights abusers are sanctionable not just by the United States but also by the EU. This will drive home the point that it is not only the United States that takes issue with Iran's illicit conduct and continues to sanction Iran.

Furthermore, U.S. officials should emphasize that when foreign firms face problems in doing business with Iran, deceptive practices by Iranian companies are to blame. The U.S. mantra should be that the more Iran complies with international norms, the easier will be its integration into the world economy. Whenever Iranian officials complain about hindered access to the international financial system, Washington should quickly respond that Tehran must first comply with the multinational Financial Action Task Force (FATF) standards on combating money laundering and terrorist financing.[5] Indeed, U.S. officials should point out that Iran must act quickly not only to meet FATF standards but also to adopt Basel III requirements established over the past five years, including on transparency in financial accounts. Further, if Iran expects to have normal transactions with foreign banks, it needs to allow for information sharing on tax compliance in line with U.S. Foreign Account Tax Compliance Act (FATCA) requirements and now the OECD-sponsored Common Reporting Standard System adopted by more than a hundred countries.[6] Whenever Iranian officials cite third-country concerns about U.S. penalties, Washington should respond that transparency from Iranian firms about their ownership would permit foreign businesses to easily comply with U.S. rules to avoid businesses affiliated with Iran's Islamic Revolutionary Guard Corps (IRGC).

Rather than talking about the sanctions that have been lifted, U.S. officials should emphasize the sanctions that remain. In citing the JCPOA chapter and verse, Washington can point to text that underscores the risks of Iranian misbehavior: the retention of sanctions authorities (sanctions are waived or suspended, not terminated) and potential for snapback; the limited list of sanctions removed, clearly indicating many remaining nonnuclear sanctions;[7] and footnotes that allow for abrogation of OFAC licenses should Iran misuse licensed aircraft.[8] Washington should then articulate that the flip side of its pledge not to introduce new nuclear sanctions is its reserved right to impose new sanctions for nonnuclear reasons. Such an approach lines up with the guiding principle suggested thus far: that the U.S. narrative should eschew a focus on sanctions going away while making clear that new sanctions do not represent a violation.

FULLY IMPLEMENT EXISTING SANCTIONS

The second element of the multipronged strategy is to intensify implementation of existing sanctions, since on a number of fronts, the Obama administration had been soft-pedaling the implementation of the existing sanctions designations.

Terrorism

More-vigorous action is needed against several Iran-sponsored entities subject to sanctions for involvement in terrorism.

First is the Qods Force (QF), the branch of the IRGC responsible for external operations and support to terrorist proxies. The QF has been Iran's primary means of providing training materials and financial support to proxies worldwide, including in the Middle East (Lebanon, Syria, Iraq, Yemen) but also beyond (e.g., Nigeria, Kenya, Latin America). New designations under existing counterterrorism executive authorities could target QF personnel and support networks, such as those in Lebanon, Syria and Yemen, as well as outside the region, such as in sub-Saharan Africa and Latin America. For example, Kenyan officials arrested two Iranians in late November 2016 outside the Israeli embassy in Nairobi, where they reportedly had been casing the facility. The two Iranians, in a vehicle with diplomatic plates, had just visited a prison where two other Iranians were being held on terrorism-related charges. According to Kenyan officials, the two jailed Iranians belong to the Qods Force, and were convicted on charges of plotting attacks against Western interests in Kenya in 2013.[9] Diplomatic engagements should also include efforts to enforce UN travel bans on QF-affiliated individuals, including its commander, Qasem Soleimani.[10]

Second is Mahan Air, which was designated in 2011 for providing support to the QF. Targeting such QF-related sanctions evaders—agents and financial fronts—would expose and disrupt networks that facilitate the QF's provision of assistance to Iranian proxies. Mahan Air continues to fly routinely to Syria,[11] possibly ferrying fighters and weapons. The airline also briefly made passenger flights from Tehran to Sana in the spring of 2015, not long after Houthi rebels took control of the Yemeni capital. These continued until the Saudi-led coalition bombed the tarmac to prevent a Mahan plane from landing.[12, 13] Despite remaining on U.S. sanctions lists, Mahan Air has opened new routes to Moscow, Kiev, Copenhagen, and Paris since January 2016.[14] The airline now reportedly flies to forty-three cities in twenty-nine countries, excluding Iran.[15]

The United States has taken only limited actions to highlight the risks of doing business with Mahan Air. In 2012, the U.S. Department of the Treasury attached sanctions to 117 aircraft belonging to Iran Air, Mahan Air, and Yas Air, alleging that Tehran was sending both Iran Air and Mahan Air flights to Damascus to deliver military and crowd-control equipment to the Assad regime.[16] Although the Iran

Air planes were removed from sanctions lists as part of the JCPOA, more than forty Mahan Air and Yas Air planes remain subject to U.S. sanctions, and as a result, foreign banks that deal with them risk losing access to the U.S. financial system. This risk applies not just to the aircraft but also to any dealings with the airline as a whole. In May 2015, the United States designated Iraq-based Al-Naser Airlines,[17] from which Mahan obtained nine aircraft, and in March 2016 designated Britain- and UAE-based front companies acting on Mahan's behalf.[18] In using sanctions authorities to expose Mahan's illicit activities and agents operating worldwide, the United States would support diplomatic efforts to encourage European, Asian, and Middle East states to ban Mahan flights, as Saudi Arabia did in April 2016,[19] as well as put pressure on commercial actors to curtail relationships with Mahan, considering the additional sanctions risks. For example, such efforts could entail public exposure through designation of intermediaries that provide Mahan ticketing and other financial services in Europe and Asia, where banks would be unlikely to work directly with Mahan given the risk of losing access to the U.S. financial system.

Third on the list of entities against which additional enforcement is needed is Hezbollah. The Hezbollah International Financing Prevention Act (HIFPA), which came into effect in March 2016, extends to Hezbollah secondary sanctions like those employed against Iran. Prior to HIFPA, a series of U.S. actions had already constrained Hezbollah's financial operations, and the new law has intensified the pressure. The Treasury Department assessed in July 2016 that Hezbollah is in "its worst financial shape in decades."[20] For his part, in a televised address the previous month, Hezbollah secretary-general Hassan Nasrallah had denied the impact of outside pressure on the organization's commercial and criminal ties, insisting that Hezbollah was funded solely by Iran. This was despite the bombing of a Lebanese bank earlier that month, widely believed to have been carried out by Hezbollah in response to the closure of reportedly hundreds of Hezbollah-related accounts by Lebanese banks, some of them arguably acting beyond the scope of the new U.S. law. While Lebanese regulatory authorities intervened to prevent so-called overcompliance with the U.S. law by local banks and forestall further confrontation with Hezbollah, additional U.S. designations of Hezbollah businessmen and businesses would give Lebanese banks cover to protect the Lebanese financial system from further abuse. Likewise, applying secondary sanctions under HIFPA to a financial institution banking Hezbollah or its associates outside the Middle East, such as in Africa or Latin America, would emphasize HIFPA's global reach and minimize the impact on Lebanon's financial sector.

Furthermore, investigations by U.S. and European law enforcement led to the revelation that Hezbollah's terrorist wing, the External Security Organization (aka the Islamic Jihad Organization), runs a dedicated entity specializing in worldwide drug trafficking and money laundering. This finding was made public in early 2016 by a joint operation that included the Drug Enforcement Administration (DEA), Customs and Border Protection, the Treasury Department, Europol, Eurojust, and authorities in France, Germany, Italy, and Belgium. The investigation spanned seven countries and led to the arrest of several members of Hezbollah's so-called Business Affairs Component (BAC) on charges of drug trafficking, money laundering, and procuring weapons for use in Syria.[21]

As a result of this transnational investigation, authorities arrested "top leaders" of the BAC's "European cell." These included Mohamad Noureddine, "a Lebanese money launderer who has worked directly with Hezbollah's financial apparatus to transfer Hezbollah funds" through his companies while maintaining "direct ties to Hezbollah commercial and terrorist elements in both Lebanon and Iraq." In January 2016, the Treasury Department had designated Noureddine and his partner, Hamdi Zaher El Dine, as Hezbollah terrorist operatives, noting that the group needs individuals like these "to launder criminal proceeds for use in terrorism and political destabilization."

The outing of the BAC resulted from a series of DEA cases run under the rubric of "Project Cassandra," which targeted "a global Hezbollah network responsible for the movement of large quantities of cocaine in the United States and Europe." But there are many other recent cases in which transnational organized criminal activities are carried out by people with formal, even senior ties to the group.

Consider the two operatives arrested in October 2015 for conspiring to launder narcotics proceeds and international arms trafficking on behalf of Hezbollah. Iman Kobeissi, arrested in Atlanta, had offered to launder drug money for an undercover agent and informed him that her associates in Hezbollah were seeking to purchase cocaine, weapons, and ammunition. Joseph Asmar, arrested in Paris the same day in a coordinated operation, also discussed potential narcotics transactions with an undercover agent, offering to use his connections with Hezbollah to provide security for drug shipments. In total, the suspects mentioned criminal contacts in at least ten countries around the world, highlighting the transnational nature of this Hezbollah-run operation.

Indeed, over the past eighteen months, the group's criminal facilitators have been arrested around the world, from Lithuania to Colombia and many points in between. Others have been designated by the Treasury Department, including Kassem Hejeij, a businessman with direct ties to Hezbollah; Husayn Ali Faour, a member of the Islamic Jihad Organization; and Abd Al Nur Shalan, a key Hezbollah weapons procurer who has close ties with the group's leadership. In the words of a senior Treasury official, "Hezbollah is using so-called legitimate businesses to fund, equip, and organize [its] subversive activities."

Under the Obama administration, however, these investigations were tamped down for fear of rocking the boat with Iran and jeopardizing the nuclear deal. Now, the Trump administration should aggressively target Hezbollah's financial, logistical, and procurement networks, including resurrecting the DEA's now-defunct Project Cassandra. The new administration should also pursue Hezbollah's BAC operatives with designations and arrests, as well as seek extradition of arrested Hezbollah facilitators in France, Colombia, Lithuania, and elsewhere, and thereafter indict them in U.S. courts.

Ballistic Missile Development and Conventional Arms Exports

Extension of ballistic missile and conventional arms restrictions on Iran for eight and five years, respectively, falls under UN Security Council Resolution 2231. Although UNSCR 2231 endorsed the JCPOA, Iran has said that it is bound only by the JCPOA and not the UN missile or arms restrictions, which it has long maintained are illegal. Since the JCPOA's implementation in January 2016, Iran has tested missiles on at least three separate occasions, most recently on January 29, 2017.[22] While UNSCR 2231 calls on Iran only to refrain from ballistic missile development—technically falling short of a ban—the resolution maintains sanctions, for the duration of the restrictions, on a number of Iranian individuals and entities involved in the country's ballistic missile program and arms exports. It also allows for new sanctions against those who act on behalf of those who remain on the list.

In addition to the remaining UN restrictions, U.S. sanctions continue to apply to a number of Iranian individuals and entities under Executive Order 13382, which applies financial sanctions to those involved in proliferation activities and their support networks.[23] Such nonproliferation sanctions can have a profound disruptive impact, since illicit procurement is often done under the guise of legitimate purchases of dual-use goods. These restrictions, however, have little meaning unless new entities are continuously added to the list of designated companies; otherwise, Iran will just create new shell fronts through which to evade the restrictions. The February 3, 2017, designation of several networks and supporters of Iran's ballistic missile procurement were the first such actions since the January 2016 designation of Mabrooka Trading for its role in missile-related procurement networks. In addition to targeting previously unknown or nonpublic fronts, robust implementation of nonproliferation sanctions ought to include continuing to identify affiliates of Iran's missile development complex, subagencies and commercial actors affiliated with the Ministry of Defense and Armed Forces Logistics (MODAFL), the Defense Industries Organization, the Aerospace Industries Organization, which has done much of their missile work, and other key missile entities, including Shahid Hemmat Industrial Group and Shahid Bakeri Industrial Group, along with additional Iranian officials cooperating with North Korea on missile development. The March 2016 sanctions that targeted subsidiaries of Shahid Hemmat Industrial and the IRGC Al-Ghadir Missile Command provide an example.[24]

Under the arms embargo of Security Council resolution 1747, adopted in March 2007, a number of Iranian individuals and entities were subjected to UN asset freezes and travel bans. These listings are maintained under the UNSCR 2231 regime. Notably, in 2012, Ali Akbar Tabatabaei, the commander of the IRGC-QF Africa Corps, was designated for overseeing weapons transfers in Africa, including a shipment intended for the Gambia by another sanctioned QF official, Hosein Aghajani.[25] The United States and UN also designated the earlier-mentioned Iranian cargo carrier Yas Air the same year for working with Hezbollah and Syrian officials to transfer weapons to Syria and the Tehran-based Behineh Trading Company for facilitating the entry of weapons and QF personnel into Nigeria.[26] In continuously updating these lists as new information becomes available, the United States must especially monitor Iranian arms transfers to Hezbollah in Syria and Houthi rebels in Yemen, and press for UN action in cases where sufficient evidence can be made public.

Human Rights Abuses

Beginning in 2010 and lasting through 2014, the United States levied a number of sanctions against Iranian commercial and governmental entities and officials for committing "serious human rights abuses" linked to the crackdown following the Iranian election in 2009. Among those sanctioned was the IRGC for the mistreatment of political detainees held in a ward of Tehran's Evin Prison, which operates under the Guards' control.[27] The sanctions also extended to the Basij and Iran's Law Enforcement Force, as well as to a number of senior security officials and government-related technology and telecommunications entities. However, no new human-rights-related designations have been made since implementation of the JCPOA.

Likewise, the EU has adopted a number of restrictive measures, including asset freezes and visa bans on individuals and entities responsible for committing human rights violations, as well as export bans on equipment that can be used for internal repression and monitoring telecommunications. Notably, the EU recently extended until April 2017 travel bans and asset freezes on eighty-two Iranian officials for their involvement in human rights violations.[28] The new administration should consider additional designations to draw attention to Iran's poor human rights record and shore up EU support to maintain human-rights-related sanctions. (The EU must extend the restrictions annually.)

The Islamic Revolutionary Guards Corps

The IRGC controls a large portion of the country's economy,[29] and a number of its affiliates remain subject to U.S. and EU sanctions. As such, the application of U.S. secondary sanctions for dealings with IRGC affiliates remains a significant risk for companies looking to reengage with Iran. The engineering company Khatam al-Anbia (KACH) and a number of its subsidiaries, such as Sepanir Oil and Gas, which serves as the general contractor for part of the South Pars gas field, also remain on the UN sanctions list based on KACH's involvement in the construction of uranium enrichment sites at the Fordow enrichment plant.[30]

The United States, however, has yet to impose secondary sanctions for dealings with the IRGC. Testifying at a hearing before the House Committee on Foreign Affairs on February 11, 2016, John Smith, the acting director of OFAC, said that he was not aware of any violations of U.S. sanctions targeting the IRGC since JCPOA implementation.[31] To be sure, the legal threshold for applying secondary sanctions is actually quite high: while an IRGC affiliate need not be listed by OFAC to create exposure for banks (it only needs to have more than 50 percent IRGC ownership), the banks must have "knowingly" engaged in a "significant transaction" to qualify for sanctions. The IRGC can exploit this standard by establishing front companies and hiding ownership or subsidiaries through nontransparent structures, making it nearly impossible for foreign companies to identify the true beneficial ownership of their counterparty.

When it comes to strengthening implementation of sanctions against the IRGC, the United States could take several steps. First, the Treasury Department can and should designate additional IRGC subsidiaries and front companies, based on either IRGC ownership or control, under existing executive orders. Independent researchers have already identified dozens of unlisted IRGC affiliates based on publicly available information.[32] Second, either executive or congressional action could be taken to lower the ownership threshold. Such a move, however, would put a greater onus on banks to identify the IRGC affiliates blocked by "operation of law" but not included on published sanctions lists, which will remain a challenge as long as Iranian financial and commercial sectors lack greater transparency. Third, Congress has raised the specter of designating the IRGC a foreign terrorist organization (FTO). Legislation introduced by Sen. Ted Cruz (R-TX) in early January 2017 calls on the State Department to assess the IRGC's suitability for designation as an FTO.[33] While there is no doubt that elements of the IRGC, such as the Qods Force, have engaged in support for terrorism, a designation would do little to strengthen sanctions against the IRGC, since it has already been designated under other authorities. Moreover, such a move is unlikely to curry international support.

Strict Enforcement of SEC Reporting Requirements

While the JCPOA allows firms to conduct a variety of new types of business with Iran, the nuclear deal does not change the requirement that firms report to the U.S. government about their business with Iran. This fact needs to be brought vigorously to the attention of foreign firms, which must hear that failure to file the required reports will result in severe penalties. Disclosure of such ties, even if legally acceptable, could also trigger state-level divestment laws.

The reporting clause for business activities in Iran is located in Section 219 of the Securities and Exchange Commission (SEC) disclosure requirements, as mandated by the 2012 Iran Threat Reduction Act, with these requirements unaffected by the JCPOA.[34] Section 219 does not prohibit any conduct, but instead requires that issuers of publicly traded securities disclose in reports filed with the SEC any transaction with any part of the Iranian government, including the Central Bank; activities supporting the Iranian petroleum industry; facilitation of transactions with the IRGC; and transactions with persons sanctioned due to terrorism or weapons proliferations reasons.[35] Note that Section 219 applies not only to issuers of publicly traded securities but also to their "affiliates," which include joint ventures, foreign-registered subsidiaries, and controlling shareholders. Likewise, Section 219 contains no "materiality" threshold, meaning that it applies to all activities, no matter how small. Since Section 219 was imposed, firms from Brazil, China, India, Japan, Britain, Switzerland, and Turkey, among other countries, have filed more than a thousand reports.

Because Section 219 disclosure requirements remain in effect, any firm with publicly traded securities in the United States will face increased reporting requirements if that firm does business with Iran. For instance, European firms previously forbidden from buying Iranian crude oil may decide to restart such purchases; if so, Section 219 disclosure requirements will be triggered. At first, the SEC Office of Global Security Risk rigorously enforced Section 219, querying companies about disclosures that omitted information about potential activities with Iran suggested by press reports. The SEC should resume such rigorous enforcement.

CONSIDER NEW NONNUCLEAR SANCTIONS

In addition to more rigorously enforcing existing sanctions, the Trump administration should impose additional nonnuclear sanctions, especially for new transgressions by Iran. Even though the United States never pledged to refrain from applying nonnuclear sanctions for Iran's ongoing activities, linking new sanctions to Iran's post-JCPOA behavior may make it easier for Washington to gain international understanding that these new sanctions are nonnuclear rather than a rebranding of the older nuclear sanctions.

Cyber Sanctions

Cyber is emerging as a key tool in Iran's arsenal for dealing with both domestic and foreign threats.[36] Beyond the use of cyber tools for repression and monitoring of domestic opposition, a number of foreign attacks have been attributed to Iran in recent years. In August 2012, malware connected to Iran by U.S. intelligence officials destroyed data and disabled tens of thousands of Saudi Aramco computers.[37] The following month, hackers with ties to the Iranian government conducted a series of denial-of-service attacks primarily targeting the U.S. financial system, according to a March 2016 indictment of seven of the hackers.[38] List-based blocking sanctions put in place by authorities under Executive Order 13694 of April 1, 2015, allow for targeting of "significant malicious cyber-enabled activities." The authority, which was recently amended and deployed against Russian targets involved in cyber interference in the U.S. election, focused on the specific harms caused by significant malicious cyber-enabled activities, including threats to national security and critical infrastructure. Application of these sanctions could be used to expose Iranian entities involved in cyberattacks and create a possible deterrent to certain quasi-governmental and commercial actors within Iran, as well as foreign partners, from assisting in further development of Iranian offensive cyber capabilities.

Money Laundering

Another possible tool is the "311" finding of Iran as a jurisdiction of primary money-laundering concern. The 311 (which refers to Section 311 of the USA PATRIOT Act) authorizes the treasury secretary to pursue a range of measures against a financial institution, jurisdiction, or class of transaction found to be of "primary money-laundering concern." Associated with the finding against Iran in 2011, the Treasury Department issued a "notice of proposed rulemaking" calling for imposition of the "fifth special measure," which would require U.S. financial institutions to implement additional due diligence to prevent improper indirect access to the U.S. financial system by Iran or Iranian entities. The finding was based on "Iran's support for terrorism; pursuit of weapons of mass destruction (WMD); reliance on state-owned or controlled agencies to facilitate WMD proliferation; and the illicit and deceptive financial activities that Iranian financial institutions—including the Central Bank of Iran—and other state-controlled entities engage in to facilitate Iran's illicit conduct and evade sanctions."[39] There is little reason to believe that Iran's illicit financial conduct has ceased under the JCPOA. However, such regulatory measures are only implemented once a final rule has been issued, which was not done for the 311 on Iran. One option would be to make clear that this is a real option should FATF, the international standard-setting body for AML/CFT, remove Iran from its blacklist in June 2017 without Iran fulfilling the mutually agreed-on reforms under its FATF action plan.

Commerce Authorities

Somewhere between more rigorous implementation of existing restrictions and adoption of new sanctions would be fuller use of export controls. In part, this would mean devoting more resources and high-level attention to enforcing existing export controls. Generally speaking, this area gets woefully little attention and money because of the faulty perception that strict enforcement will cost U.S. jobs, when in fact most U.S. firms avoid questionable transactions. Thus, tighter enforcement will primarily affect foreign firms that incorporate U.S. products or technology in what they sell. In addition, it may well be appropriate to tighten export controls on products bound for Iran, such as products Iran is using for its cyberwarfare activities. Just by playing up export controls and their application to goods with more than 10 percent U.S.-origin content, the U.S. government could have a considerable chilling effect on those considering selling dual-use items to Iran. In sum, compliance with export controls is so complicated and resource-intensive that it is an underappreciated deterrent to commercial actors.

APPLY PROPORTIONAL SANCTIONS FOR JCPOA NONCOMPLIANCE

When Congress was considering the nuclear deal, the Obama administration insisted that it had reserved the right to apply proportional sanctions in the event of Iranian noncompliance with parts of the deal—that is, snapback of sanctions would not be an all-or-nothing proposition, nor would it depend on reaching consensus with the other major powers on whether Iran was complying with the deal's provisions. Adam Szubin, acting undersecretary of the treasury for terrorism and financial intelligence, acknowledged the concerns of international partners regarding minor violations by Iran when he noted in December 2015 that "we retain full flexibility, from partial measures to total snap back..."[40] That flexibility, the Obama team insisted, showed that the threat of snapback sanctions was real, rather than a purely theoretical provision.

Unfortunately, Iran may well not be complying with a part of the deal—not violating the deal so openly that the other major powers will agree that a full sanctions snapback is required but nevertheless calling for a firm U.S. response. In particular, Iran has made limited use of the nuclear procurement mechanism, set up by the JCPOA, through which Iran is supposed to acquire all foreign materials for its enrichment program. As of mid-January 2017, the mechanism had received only five requests to provide restricted goods to Iran, three of which had been approved and two that remained pending with the UN Security Council.[41] It is implausible that a nuclear program the size and scope of Iran's would need little from abroad. Indeed, the German government reported in summer 2016 that Iran continued to procure material for its nuclear program through other channels.[42] Washington should therefore insist on a discussion in the Joint Commission about Iran's obligations regarding this procurement mechanism. In its current approach, Iran claims no obligation to follow this mechanism, asserting the obligation belongs entirely to the government of the country where the supplier is located (this was also the Obama administration's interpretation). The Trump administration should devote intelligence community resources to identifying Iranian procurement occurring outside this mechanism.

Should clear evidence emerge indicating Iran is avoiding its obligations to use the procurement channel, Washington has the right under the agreement to trigger the mechanisms for full reimposition of nuclear sanctions. However, such a move would be an extreme reaction to a limited violation, and other countries quite possibly might not go along—helping explain why the nuclear deal's critics said the snapback provisions were unlikely to be invoked. Altogether, the United States should make clear that it reserves the right to impose appropriate sanctions even in the absence of international agreement on how to respond. Washington here needs to show that it does indeed reserve the right to act unilaterally against limited Iranian noncompliance: snapback is not all-or-nothing, nor is it contingent on complete agreement within the international community. The Obama administration claimed to be contemplating such unilateral and limited action in the case of limited Iranian noncompliance, so the Trump administration would be on firm ground adopting such a policy.

CONCLUSION

The new administration should develop, articulate, and implement a clear post-JCPOA sanctions policy based on the elements laid out in this paper: emphasizing the sanctions that remain; fully implementing those sanctions; and developing new nonnuclear sanctions and proportional responses to Iranian noncompliance with the JCPOA.

Allowing Iran to continue defining the success of the nuclear deal in terms of insufficient trade resumed or difficulty of financing obscures the role of Iran's nonnuclear behavior in dispelling potential commercial partners. Such behavior includes Iran's failure to abide by international norms both in moderating aggressive behavior in the region and in implementing reforms protecting its financial and commercial sectors from illicit financial activity and sanctions evasion. The Trump administration should therefore focus on Iran's conduct as the reason for the country's continuing isolation and the basis for a resumption of financial pressures.

While the administration has broad authority to shape sanctions policy and implementation, not all options are implementable, advisable, or should be employed immediately. First, there are limits to U.S. jurisdiction and the ability to compel foreign compliance. Consequently, policy should focus on building a broad coalition based on the consensus that Iranian behavior violates international norms. This is not to say that unilateral sanctions are useless. They can serve to communicate Iranian illicit activity and cause commercial actors to withdraw voluntarily from business based on reputational concerns, creating political openings for third countries to act. Second, Iran-specific changes to principles that underlie broader sanctions policy would complicate implementation. In such a case, direct action under existing authorities or the creation of new authorities is preferable to modifying guidance or enforcement. Finally, Congress is going to want to play a role in strengthening the role of sanctions in restraining Iran. The new administration and congress will need to work together to ensure that they are moving in the same direction.

KATHERINE BAUER, the Blumenstein-Katz Family Fellow at The Washington Institute, is a former Treasury official who served as the department's financial attaché in Jerusalem and the Gulf. She also served as the senior policy advisor for Iran and assistant director in the Office of Terrorist Financing and Financial Crimes.

NOTES

1. See http://washin.st/pnote38

2. "Treasury Sanctions Those Involved in Ballistic Missile Procurement for Iran," January 17, 2016, https://www.treasury.gov/press-center/press-releases/Pages/jl0322.aspx

3. "Iran Says Kerry's Remarks on Sanctions 'Unacceptable,'" *Gulf News*, October 17, 2016, http://gulfnews.com/news/mena/iran/iran-says-kerry-s-remarks-on-sanctions-unacceptable-1.1913911.

4. Kristina Wong, "U.S. General Sees 'Uptick' in Bad Behavior by Iran since Nuke Deal," *The Hill*, November 30, 2016, http://thehill.com/policy/defense/308151-us-general-sees-uptick-in-malign-iranian-activities-since-nuclear-deal#.WFBMCi_bCe4.twitter.

5. For more, see Katherine Bauer, "Iran Faces Challenges in Implementing Its FATF Action Plan," PolicyWatch 2717 (Washington Institute for Near East Policy, October 26, 2016), http://www.washingtoninstitute.org/policy-analysis/view/iran-faces-challenges-in-implementing-its-fatf-action-plan; see also Matthew Levitt and Katherine Bauer, "Iran's 'Resistance Economy'—and Stalled Reform Efforts," *Wall Street Journal*, September 23, 2016, http://blogs.wsj.com/washwire/2016/09/23/irans%E2%80%8B-resistance-economy-and-stalled-reform-efforts/?cb=logged0.8635195400458011.

6. Known formally as the Standard for Automatic Exchange of Financial Account Information, under the Convention on Mutual Administrative Assistance in Tax Matters. Some of the one hundred countries will begin the automatic exchange only in 2018.

7. JCPOA Annex II (about sanctions-lifting), Part B (what the U.S. government will do), Section 4.1.1., in which the deal expressly notes the U.S. pledge to cease applying sanctions on certain designated individuals and entities subject to sanctions under the Comprehensive Iran Sanctions, Accountability, and Divestment Act of 2010 (CISADA). The United States did not commit to lift CISADA. In fact, it is because CISADA still remains in effect that secondary sanctions apply to Iran-related individuals and entities designated under nonnuclear authorities.

8. JCPOA Annex II, Part B, footnote 12: "Should the United States determine that licensed aircraft, goods, or services have been used for purposes other than exclusively civil aviation end-use, or have been re-sold or re-transferred to persons on the SDN List, the United States would view this as grounds to cease performing its commitments under Section 5.1.1 in whole or in part." In other words, the consequence of using planes for anything other than "exclusively civil aviation end-use" is expressly written into the JCPOA.

9. Tom Odula, "Two Iranians Charged in Kenyan Court with Terrorism," Associated Press, December 1, 2016, http://bigstory.ap.org/article/baa8add6425841a9b54efb7f8bd56850/2-iranians-charged-kenyan-court-terrorism.

10. "The List Established and Maintained pursuant to Security Council Res. 2231 (2015)," United Nations, https://scsanctions.un.org/fop/fop?xml=htdocs/resources/xml/en/consolidated.xml&xslt=htdocs/resources/xsl/en/iran.xsl.

11. Emanuele Ottolenghi, "Flying in the Face of U.S. Sanctions," *Wall Street Journal*, February 3, 2016, http://www.wsj.com/articles/flying-in-the-face-of-u-s-sanctions-1454531168.

12. "First Iran Flight Lands in Shiite-Held Yemen Capital," *National*, March 1, 2015, http://www.thenational.ae/world/middle-east/first-iran-flight-lands-in-shiite-held-yemen-capital.

13. Mohammed Ali Kalfood and Kareem Fahim, "Saudis Hit a Yemeni Airport, Possibly Closing Aid Route," *New York Times*, April 28, 2015, http://www.nytimes.com/2015/04/29/world/middleeast/saudis-hit-a-yemeni-airport-possibly-closing-aid-route.html.

14. See Mahan Air Press Room, http://www.mahan.aero/en/contact/press-room.

15. See Mahan Air International Route Network, http://www.mahan.aero/en/destinations/route-network.

16. U.S. Department of the Treasury, "Treasury Designates Syrian Entity, Others Involved in Arms and Communications Procurement Networks and Identifies Blocked Iranian Aircraft," press release, September 19, 2012, https://www.treasury.gov/press-center/press-releases/Pages/tg1714.aspx.

17. U.S. Department of the Treasury, "Treasury Department Targets Those Involved in Iranian Scheme to Purchase Airplanes," press release, May 21, 2015, https://www.treasury.gov/press-center/press-releases/Pages/jl10061.aspx.

18. U.S. Department of the Treasury, "Treasury Sanctions Supporters of Iran's Ballistic Missile Program and Terrorism-Designated Mahan Air," press release, March 24, 2016, https://www.treasury.gov/press-center/press-releases/Pages/jl0395.aspx.

19. Sami Aboudi, "Saudi Arabia Suspends Iran's Mahan Air License to Use Its Air Space," Reuters, April 4, 2016, http://www.reuters.com/article/us-saudi-iran-aviation-idUSKCN0X123L.

20. U.S. Department of the Treasury, "Testimony of Acting Under Secretary for Terrorism and Financial Intelligence Adam J. Szubin before the House Committee on Foreign Affairs," press release, May 25, 2016, https://www.treasury.gov/press-center/press-releases/Pages/jl0466.aspx.

21. U.S. Drug Enforcement Administration, "DEA and European Authorities Uncover Massive Hizballah Drug and Money Laundering Scheme," February 1, 2016, https://www.dea.gov/divisions/hq/2016/hq020116.shtml.

22. Peter Kenyon, "Did Iran's Ballistic Missile Test Violate A U.N. Resolution?" *NPR Parallels*, February 3, 2017, http://www.npr.org/sections/parallels/2017/02/03/513229839/did-irans-ballistic-missile-test-violate-a-u-n-resolution.

23. U.S. Department of State, "Executive Order 13382—Blocking Property of Weapons of Mass Destruction Proliferators and Their Supporters," July 1, 2005, http://www.state.gov/documents/organization/135435.pdf.

24. U.S. Department of the Treasury, "Treasury Sanctions Supporters of Iran's Ballistic Missile Program and Terrorism-Designated Mahan Air," press release, March 24, 2016, https://www.treasury.gov/press-center/press-releases/Pages/jl0395.aspx.

25. U.S. Department of the Treasury, "Treasury Targets Iranian Arms Shipments," press release, March 27, 2012, https://www.treasury.gov/press-center/press-releases/Pages/tg1506.aspx.

26. Ibid.

27. U.S. Department of the Treasury, "Treasury Sanctions Iranian Security Forces for Human Rights Abuses," press release, June 9, 2011, https://www.treasury.gov/press-center/press-releases/Pages/tg1204.aspx.

28. "Council Decision (CFSP) 2016/565 Amending Decision 2011/235/CFSP concerning Restrictive Measures Directed against Certain Persons and Entities in View of the Situation in Iran," *Official Journal of the European Union*, April 12, 2016, http://eur-lex.europa.eu/legal-content/EN/TXT/PDF/?uri=CELEX:32016D0565&qid=1460465337598&from=EN.

29. Greg Bruno, Jayshree Bajoria, and Jonathan Masters, "Iran's Revolutionary Guards," *CFR Backgrounder*, Council on Foreign Relations, June 14, 2013, http://www.cfr.org/iran/irans-revolutionary-guards/p14324.

30. United Nations, "Security Council Imposes Additional Sanctions on Iran, Voting 12 in Favour to 2 Against, with 1 Abstention," June 9, 2010, http://www.un.org/press/en/2010/sc9948.doc.htm.

31. "Iran Nuclear Deal Oversight: Implementation and Its Consequences," hearing before the Committee on Foreign Affairs, U.S. House of Representatives, February 11, 2016, http://docs.house.gov/meetings/FA/FA00/20160211/104456/HHRG-114-FA00-Transcript-20160211.pdf.

32. See Annex I of 2015 testimony by Emanuele Ottolenghi before the House Committee on Foreign Affairs for a list of publicly traded companies in which the IRGC is a shareholder. The document contains active links to Tehran Stock Exchange ownership information. As Ottolenghi notes in his testimony, in a number of cases, ostensible ownership is held by undesignated IRGC affiliates whereas effective ownership and control by designated individuals or entities is obscured through the chain of fronts: "The Iran Nuclear Deal and Its Impact on Iran's Islamic Revolutionary Guard Corps," September 17, 2015, http://www.defenddemocracy.org/content/uploads/documents/Ottolenghi_HFAC_IranDeal_IRGC.pdf.

33. U.S. Senate Foreign Relations Committee, "S.67—A bill to direct the secretary of state to submit to Congress a report on the designation of Iran's Revolutionary Guard Corps as a Foreign Terrorist Organization, and for other purposes," 115th Congress (2017–18), https://www.congress.gov/bill/115th-congress/senate-bill/67/text?q=%7B%22search%22%3A%5B%22S.67%22%5D%7D&r=1.

34. This discussion of Section 219 draws heavily on Marik String and David Horn, "As Iran Sanctions Wane, SEC Reporting Will Not," *Securities Regulation & Law Report*, January 2016, available at https://www.wilmerhale.com/uploadedFiles/Shared_Content/Editorial/Publications/Documents/2016-01-26-Bloomberg-BNA-As-Iran-Sanctions-Wane-SEC-Reporting-Will-Not.pdf.

35. In a further complication for compliance, Section 219 exempts from disclosure dealings with the government of Iran if undertaken pursuant to a U.S. government license. It is not clear if that includes the general licenses issues by OFAC; see https://www.treasury.gov/resource-center/sanctions/Documents/hr_1905_pl_112_158.pdf, p. 22.

36. See Michael Eisenstadt, *Iran's Lengthening Cyber Shadow*, Research Note 34 (Washington DC: Washington Institute, 2016), http://www.washingtoninstitute.org/uploads/Documents/pubs/ResearchNote34_Eisenstadt.pdf.

37. Nicole Perlroth, "In Cyberattack on Saudi Firm, U.S. Sees Iran Firing Back," *New York Times*, October 23, 2016, http://www.nytimes.com/2012/10/24/business/global/cyberattack-on-saudi-oil-firm-disquiets-us.html.

38. Dustin Volz and Jim Finkle, "U.S. Indicts Iranians for Hacking Dozens of Banks, New York Dam," Reuters, March 25, 2016, http://www.reuters.com/article/us-usa-iran-cyber-idUSKCN0WQ1JF.

39. U.S. Department of the Treasury, "Fact Sheet: New Sanctions on Iran," press release, November 21, 2011, https://www.treasury.gov/press-center/press-releases/Pages/tg1367.aspx.

40. U.S. Department of the Treasury, "Remarks by Acting Under Secretary for Terrorism and Financial Intelligence Adam Szubin at the Atlantic Council and the Iran Project Symposium," press release, December 17, 2015, https://www.treasury.gov/press-center/press-releases/Pages/jl0304.aspx.

41. United Nations, Second report of the Secretary-General on the implementation of Security Council resolution 2231 (2015), 30 December 2016, http://www.un.org/ga/search/view_doc.asp?symbol=S/2016/1136.

42. Ryan Browne, "German Intelligence: Iran May Have Tried to Violate Nuclear Deal," CNN, July 8, 2016, http://www.cnn.com/2016/07/08/politics/germany-iran-violate-nuclear-deal/.

Chairman ROYCE. Feel free, Mr. Albright, please.

STATEMENT OF MR. DAVID ALBRIGHT, FOUNDER AND PRESIDENT, INSTITUTE FOR SCIENCE AND INTERNATIONAL SECURITY

Mr. ALBRIGHT. Thank you, Mr. Chairman, Ranking Member, and other members of this committee for holding this hearing today and inviting me to testify. I applaud your committee's efforts to understand and chart a way forward on Iran policy.

I would like to limit my comments to the Iran nuclear deal which I would like to see maintained, but the deal must be better enforced and implemented, its nuclear conditions more strictly interpreted, its verification improved, and its short and long term deficiencies fixed. I have listed in my testimony several steps to fix the weaknesses in the deal and will discuss some of them here.

But first, I would like to talk a little bit about some of the specific problems in the deal's implementation. As the chairman mentioned, Iran continues to test nuclear-capable ballistic missiles. We can argue whether this is inconsistent with or in violation of U.N. Security Council Resolution 2231, however, the fact of the matter is that a nuclear warhead without a reliable delivery system is not a militarily useful weapon. So progress on ballistic missiles today and tomorrow represents progress toward Iran building a nuclear weapons arsenal in the future.

The workings of the deal have been far too secret. Moreover, the IAEA continues to under report the actual situation on the ground. Many of the Joint Commission decisions are questionable and I have given several examples in my testimony. Also, so far Iran has resisted IAEA inspections of military sites and the risk is growing that Iran is creating no-go zones for inspectors inside Iran. Moreover, during the JCPOA negotiations and extending for some time afterwards, the Obama administration interfered in U.S. law enforcement efforts. It blocked or did not process the extradition requests and lure memos aimed at Iranians and their agents alleged of violating U.S. trade control and sanction laws.

I would like to briefly discuss some specific steps to ensure stricter enforcement in strengthening the JCPOA in the short term, and I give many in my testimony. There is a need to achieve greater transparency in IAEA access. The U.S. and its allies should press IAEA to include greater details in its quarterly reports to the Board of Governors. Parallel agreements to the JCPOA should be publicly released. More importantly, it is critical to ensure that Iran provides guaranteed, timely IAEA access to Iranian military facilities.

It is also a priority to prevent Iran from developing an indigenous enriched uranium fuel capability. If they do so this would lay the basis for an expanded industrial scale centrifuge program that would be very difficult to stop. Toward that goal, further exemptions to the 300 kilogram enriched uranium cap should be deferred indefinitely. There are also numerous loopholes to the JCPOA that need to be fixed. I will mention two here.

The Oman loophole for heavy water should be plugged. To that end all shipments of Iranian heavy water from Oman or other overseas storage locations should be subject to approval by the Procurement Working Group. It is also important to ensure that Iran is abiding by restrictions on centrifuge R&D under the JCPOA. There are examples where they are pushing the envelope and the pushback needs to happen.

It is also critical that Iran create and implement a strategic trade control system that meets international standards. As part of creating a strategic trade control regime in Iran, the United States should also interpret the JCPOA as stating that Iran will commit not to conduct illicit commodity trafficking for government controlled or owned military, missile, nuclear, or other industries and programs.

As we await that there needs to be more effective enforcement of trading bans and sanctions. The administration should commit to more aggressively investigate, indict, and extradite those involved in outfitting Iran's nuclear missile or conventional weapons programs in defiance of U.S. laws and sanctions. The administration and its allies should step up efforts with allies to detect, interdict, or otherwise thwart Iran's illicit procurement efforts that violate national and international laws.

At the same time, the United States and its allies should take steps to better detect and block Iranian cooperation with North Korea on ballistic missiles, cruise missiles, and conventional arms. They should also devote more intelligence resources determining if North Korea and Iran are cooperating on nuclear programs or transferring nuclear or nuclear related technology, equipment, or materials.

Beyond the short term problems, the Iran deal has fundamental long term deficiencies that need to be addressed. Which problems to focus on and how to remedy them should be part of an Iran policy review by the Trump administration and Congress. Two priorities are extending the nuclear limitations in the deal and limiting Iran's ballistic missiles. One suggestion covering the former is to maintain a 12-month breakout requirement forever.

Since I have run out of time let me end there. Thank you.

[The prepared statement of Mr. Albright follows:]

Testimony of David Albright,
President of the
Institute for Science and International Security,
before the House Foreign Affairs Committee

Hearing Title: "Iran on Notice"

February 16, 2017

The Joint Comprehensive Plan of Action (JCPOA) needs to be implemented more effectively, its nuclear conditions strengthened, and its verification improved. Its implementation has been too permissive and tolerant of Iran's behavior to violate the deal, exploit loopholes, avoid critical verification requirements, and generally push the envelope of allowed behavior. Too often concessions have been made from a misplaced fear that Iran would walk away from the deal or somehow President Rouhani's presidency needed protecting. However, the deal can be better enforced by the United States without leading to its termination. As a matter of policy, the Trump administration should close key loopholes in the agreement and move to correct its short- and long-term deficiencies.

At its heart, the Iran deal is a bet that by the time the nuclear limitations end, Iran, the region, or both will have changed so much that Iran will no longer seek nuclear weapons. But despite immense sanctions relief, Iran has been increasing its conventional military power and regional hegemony, and threatening its neighbors. The bet does not appear to be winnable under the current circumstances.

Those who argued that the nuclear deal would moderate Iran's behavior in the region have sadly been disappointed. Moreover, a trade of prisoners for hostages only encouraged Iran to seize more Americans. Armed with substantial funds and a growing economy, Iran is challenging the United States in the region and appears as committed to maintaining the capability to pursue a nuclear weapons path as before, just a longer path.

When the major nuclear limitations end, Iran has stated it will have an industrial-size enrichment program, poised to break out within days or weeks. It will have developed advanced centrifuges that would enable a quick sneak out to nuclear weapons. It is mastering long-range, nuclear-capable ballistic missiles including possibly intercontinental nuclear-tipped ballistic missiles. This Iranian nuclear future is unacceptable. A solution needs to thought through and a remediation path developed.

Dealing with the short-term implementation mistakes and fixing JCPOA loopholes and deficiencies need to be priorities. Although the nuclear deal should not be abrogated, as it has many benefits, the deal must be implemented differently and strengthened.

Taking Stock of Implementation

Iran continues to test ballistic missiles that are inconsistent with, or to some in the administration, in violation of UN Security Council resolution 2231. Iran's ongoing development of missiles capable of carrying nuclear weapons is a direct threat to the nuclear deal. A nuclear weapon should be properly defined as a nuclear warhead and a delivery system. This definition was used by South Africa for its nuclear weapons program back in the 1980s, when that program was active and engaged in intense secrecy and obfuscation to deceive the world. It too denied that its missiles would ever carry nuclear weapons, a fact it admitted only after it verifiably abandoned its nuclear weapons program in the early 1990s. As the administration and Congress chart a new Iran nuclear policy, Iran's ballistic missile program should be viewed as the other half of a nuclear weapon whose development continues unabated today and should be treated accordingly.

What are some of the specific problems in the nuclear deal's implementation? First, the workings of the deal have been far too secret. Some portions of the parallel or side deals and secret Joint Commission and Procurement Working Group (PWG) decisions and actions have been publicly revealed. Although the Joint Commission decided after Donald Trump won the presidency to release its major decisions, likely feeling increasing pressure to do so, much still remains secret. Moreover, the International Atomic Energy Agency (IAEA) continues to underreport the actual situation on the ground.

Many of the Joint Commission decisions are questionable. Too much low enriched uranium (LEU) was exempted from the JCPOA 300 kilogram LEU cap, and too many hot cells in violation of the deal's size limits were allowed to continue to operate. Iran was allowed to exceed its cap of 130 metric tons of heavy water by over 70 metric tons via a loophole in the JCPOA to secretly cache heavy water in Oman while awaiting its sale.[1] A sounder interpretation of the deal, and one more in U.S. interests, would have been to apply the 130 metric ton cap to all the heavy water under Iran's control or ownership regardless of location, thereby requiring Iran to blend at least 70 metric tons of heavy water down to normal water and not ship it out to Oman in the first place.

So far, Iran has resisted IAEA inspections of military sites. Although Iran has granted access to nuclear sites, it has reportedly resisted granting access to military locations associated with past undeclared nuclear activities or potentially involved in nuclear weapons development activities banned under the JCPOA. To this day, the IAEA has not been able to state that Iran has addressed its concerns and questions about past nuclear weapons activities or to determine the exact status of what Iran achieved and may have hidden away. In addition to past activities, the IAEA has not stated that it is successfully verifying the JCPOA's prohibitions on specific nuclear weapons development activities, which would require access to military sites.

---

[1] See for example, *Heavy Water Loophole In the Iran Deal*, by David Albright and Andrea Stricker, Institute for Science and International Security Report, December 21. 2016. http://isis-online.org/isis-reports/detail/heavy-water-loophole-in-the-iran-deal

The poorly designed arrangement between Iran and the IAEA on Parchin not surprisingly failed to resolve the issue. It also put the IAEA in a weak position to move forward on accessing the Parchin site to resolve this issue, which includes making sense out of uranium particles detected by environmental sampling at Parchin. The presence of these particles combined with all the previous, suspicious site alterations is dramatic evidence that Iran conducted secret nuclear weapons activities at Parchin, despite its on-going denials.

Iran's refusal to let the IAEA resolve Parchin issues or regularly visit military sites is a major blemish on the JCPOA. It undermines any argument that the Iran deal is adequately verified.

Moreover, out of a misplaced fear of negatively affecting the deal, the Obama administration also interfered in U.S. law enforcement efforts. During the negotiations and for some time afterwards, the administration blocked or did not process several extradition requests and lure memos aimed at arresting and convicting Iranians and their agents engaged in breaking U.S. export and sanctions laws. These actions, largely concentrated in the State Department, reportedly interfered with investigations and served to discourage new or on-going federal investigations of commodity trafficking involving Iran.

The Procurement Working Group recently allowed Iran to acquire 149 metric tons of natural uranium. Iran's nuclear chief said last week that Iran would have 60 percent more stockpiled uranium than it did prior to the deal. Ali Akbar Salehi, the head of the Atomic Energy Organization of Iran, was quoted by the semi-official Fars News Agency stating that Iran would receive a final batch of 149 tons of natural uranium, in addition to 210 tons already delivered since early 2016. The 149 metric tons was a swap for sending part of its cache of heavy water in Oman to Russia, heavy water that should have been blended down into normal water instead, if the deal had been seriously enforced. Interestingly, the caching of heavy water in Oman and the decision to approve sending natural uranium to Iran were considered secret by the Joint Commission and the Obama administration. These 149 metric tons, if enriched to weapon-grade uranium, would be enough for over 15 nuclear weapons.

The Atomic Energy Organization of Iran has sought sensitive nuclear-related materials and facilities, in at least two cases knowing that the supplier country would deny the exports. Under the deal, Iran can ask for whatever it wants overseas and does not have to report it. The supplier is the one that must seek the permission from its government and the Procurement Working Group. This loophole lays the basis for secret Iranian illicit procurement efforts with less scrupulous suppliers and countries.

Mechanisms for Obtaining Improvements

There are several mechanisms to better enforce and strengthen the Iran deal both in the short and long term. The United States can take unilateral steps within the context of the JCPOA, such as by blocking proposals for goods going to Iran via the Procurement Working Group or blocking further exemptions to the 300 kilogram cap. The United States can press for strengthening measures in the Joint Commission, the executive body of the JCPOA. In fact, under U.S. leadership, the Joint Commission did strengthen the condition in the JCPOA on near 20 percent enriched uranium. The Joint Commission added a new condition that any fuel containing near

20 percent LEU would have to be irradiated; none could be stored as fresh or unirradiated fuel. Although this step of irradiating the fuel will not affect breakout timelines that significantly, it is a precedent for the ability of the Joint Commission to add conditions to the deal.

The United States can encourage the IAEA to better verify conditions in the JCPOA. There are many possibilities, including the IAEA more thoroughly monitoring the use of several large hot cells in Iran exempted for use outside JCPOA size limitations and the inspectors cracking down on Iran's attempts to push the envelope on centrifuge R&D activities. The United States can press the IAEA to use its rights to access military sites or personnel in Iran in furtherance of effective JCPOA verification. In addition, parallel agreements between Iran and the IAEA can be negotiated that enshrine the IAEA's access to Parchin or other military sites or create work plans to settle outstanding verification issues associated with reaching a broader conclusion under the Additional Protocol.

A final option is to negotiate a JCPOA II and a new UN Security Council resolution. These efforts, which would take a while to launch, could focus on repairing major weaknesses in the deal associated with the duration of the nuclear limitations and ballistic missiles.

Short Term Priorities for the Administration

The administration should announce that the United States will demonstrate zero tolerance for Iranian violations of the JCPOA, no matter how small, and will respond both within and outside the context of the JCPOA. Where violations are significant or the frequency of minor infractions reach a threshold, the United States should snap back UN sanctions.

The administration should state that it now views the following as not allowed by, and even in some cases inconsistent with, the JCPOA: (1) heavy water excess being cached overseas, e.g. in Oman, awaiting sale, (2) Iran selling any heavy water without a proposal submitted to the PWG, (3) exemptions of low enriched uranium from the 300 kilogram cap, except in extraordinary circumstances (such as for a modified Arak reactor) (4) lack of regular IAEA access to Iranian military sites, (5) enrichment of depleted uranium to natural uranium outside the 300 kilogram cap, (6) Iran not reporting to the Joint Commission about any request for nuclear or nuclear-related goods, and (7) Iranian cooperation with North Korea.

Specific Steps to Ensure Stricter Enforcement and Strengthening of the JCPOA in the Short Term

- **Achieving Greater Transparency and IAEA Access**
  - Pressing the IAEA to include greater details in its quarterly reports to the Board of Governors.[2]

---

[2] The quarterly reports should include Iran's total inventory of enriched uranium stocks and their chemical forms and how much is included in the 300 kg cap and how much exempted from this cap; Iran's quarterly enrichment production output at Natanz; status of stable isotope production efforts at Fordow and elsewhere; natural uranium production and imports; heavy water quarterly production and total inventory domestically and in Oman or other off-shore locations; status and progress in centrifuge R&D and reporting on the number of manufactured centrifuges rotor assemblies; status of construction and operation of advanced centrifuge assembly facilities at Natanz;

- o Pressing the IAEA to provide details about its plans and progress in reaching a broader conclusion and ensuring the absence of undeclared nuclear materials and activities in Iran.
- o Publicly releasing parallel agreements to the JCPOA, including Iran's long term enrichment R&D plan and the agreement regarding Iran's ability to limit inspections at Parchin.
- o Ensuring that Iran provides guaranteed, timely IAEA access to Iranian military facilities, consistent with the access timeframes in the Additional Protocol, where the IAEA suspects nuclear-related activities have occurred or it needs access to verify specified JCPOA bans on nuclear weapons development activities.

- **Preventing Iran Developing an Indigenous Enriched Uranium Fuel Fabrication Capability**
  - o Ensuring and taking steps at the Joint Commission and Procurement Working Group so that Iran does not research, develop, or import a domestic enriched uranium fuel manufacturing capability. Toward that goal, further exemptions to the 300 kilogram enriched uranium cap should be deferred indefinitely.
  - o Reviewing all civil reactor sales to Iran with the goal of ensuring that these sales include a minimum of a ten-year fuel supply that is renewable for the life of the reactor and do not include the transfer of fuel fabrication or hot cell facilities in whole or in part. The goal should be to ensure a lifetime of fuel for any reactor provided to Iran and the absence of the supply of fuel fabrication capabilities and hot cells associated with fuel development or testing.

- **Plugging Loopholes in the JCPOA**
  - o Closing the Oman loophole for heavy water. To that end, all shipments of Iranian heavy water from Oman (or other overseas storage locations) would be subject to approval by the Procurement Working Group.
  - o Banning research and development of naval reactors, including land prototypes.
  - o Closing the loophole whereby Iran enriches depleted uranium to natural uranium, unless the product (albeit natural uranium) is considered part of the 300 kilogram LEU cap.
  - o Investigating, reviewing, strictly interpreting, and ensuring Iran is abiding by restrictions on centrifuge R&D under the JCPOA. One example is allegations that Iran is exploiting allowed "quality assurance" criteria at Kalaye Electric and possibly elsewhere to conduct additional mechanical testing of centrifuges beyond that allowed under the JCPOA.

---

locations, characterizations, and monitoring of hot cells; work carried out to date on the Arak reactor; as well as other nuclear activities. The report should also discuss controversies with Iran over interpretation or implementation of JCPOA conditions and the comprehensive safeguards agreement and associated Additional Protocol, as well as progress or problems in reaching a broader conclusion.

- o Reviewing the existing conditions on near 20 percent low enriched uranium to determine their adequacy, including evaluating the raising of the radiation limit imposed on fresh LEU fuel from its current relatively low level.

- **Strengthening the Procurement Working Group**
  - o Reviewing the operation of the Procurement Working Group, including lengthening by several weeks the period for the review of submitted proposals.
  - o Requiring that Iran report any requests for nuclear or nuclear-related goods to the Joint Commission and Procurement Working Group.

- **Creating an Iranian Export Control System**
  - o Insisting that Iran create and implement a strategic trade control system that meets international standards and that will be subject to review by the Joint Commission. According to the JCPOA, "Iran *intends* to apply nuclear export policies and practices in line with the internationally established standards for the export of nuclear material, equipment and technology (emphasis added)."[3] Iran has not committed to do so, and Tehran could interpret this condition far differently than the United States. As part of creating a strategic trade control regime in Iran, the United States should also interpret the JCPOA as stating that Iran will commit not to conduct illicit commodity trafficking for government controlled or owned military, missile, nuclear, or other industries and programs, and it will agree to enforce this ban on private Iranian companies. Conducting illicit commodity trafficking is not in line with internationally established standards for strategic trade control systems.

- **Creating More Effective Enforcement of Trading Bans and Sanctions**
  - o Stepping up efforts with allies to detect, interdict, or otherwise thwart Iran's illicit procurement efforts that violate national and international laws.
  - o The Department of Justice committing to more aggressively investigating, indicting, and extraditing those involved in outfitting Iran's nuclear, missile, or conventional weapons programs in defiance of U.S. laws and sanctions. As discussed above, during the last administration, there was excessive denial or non-processing of extradition requests and lure memos out of a misplaced concern about their effect on the Iran nuclear deal. These actions, largely concentrated in the State Department, reportedly interfered with investigations and served to discourage new or on-going federal investigations of commodity trafficking involving Iran. This trend needs to be reversed by an administration-wide policy to encourage investigations of Iranian (and other pariah state) commodity trafficking efforts that includes a determined extradition process.

---

[3] JCPOA, Annex 1, par. 73: "Iran intends to apply nuclear export policies and practices in line with the internationally established standards for the export of nuclear material, equipment and technology. For 15 years, Iran will only engage, including through export of any enrichment or enrichment related equipment and technology, with any other country, or with any foreign entity in enrichment or enrichment related activities, including related research and development activities, following approval by the Joint Commission."

- o Reviewing past U.S. lure and extradition requests relating to Iran as to the feasibility and practicality of the State Department belatedly approving them.
- o Taking steps to better detect and block Iranian cooperation with North Korea on ballistic missiles, cruise missiles, and conventional arms. Devoting more intelligence resources to determining if North Korea and Iran are cooperating on nuclear programs or transferring nuclear technology, equipment, or materials.

Longer Term Improvements

The Iran deal has fundamental long-term deficiencies that need to be addressed. Which problems to focus on and how to remedy them should be part of an Iran policy review by the Trump administration. A few recommended remedies are ensuring:

- Limits on the enrichment level and a 12 month breakout requirement remain in place in perpetuity. This would involve addressing the JCPOA's phased lifting of restrictions on Iran's enrichment capabilities at year 10 and after.
- Full resolution of the outstanding issues about Iran's past secret nuclear activities, including those associated with the "possible military dimensions" of Iran's nuclear programs.
- An effective verification regime able to ensure an absence of undeclared nuclear material and facilities in Iran and adequate warning of major violations.
- Limits on Iranian ballistic missile development, testing, and production.

Conclusion

The Trump administration appears committed to maintaining the JCPOA. This decision makes good sense. But the administration also recognizes that if the deal is to survive and serve U.S. national security interests, the JCPOA needs to be more strictly enforced and interpreted, and its most significant weaknesses need to be corrected.

Chairman ROYCE. Mr. Modell.

STATEMENT OF MR. SCOTT MODELL, MANAGING DIRECTOR, THE RAPIDAN GROUP

Mr. MODELL. Chairman Royce, Ranking Member Engel, members of the committee, thank you very much for the opportunity to come back and discuss what I would call the next generation of Iran pushback. I have testified here before and I think I am in the consensus to say that the last 8 years has been overly passive.

And I have pushed forward—thinking ideas that there are ways, the tools we have and ways in which we can push back against what we often call the Iranian Action Network that have been overlooked and ignored as a result of an overly accommodating policy over the last 8 years. A lot of the recommendations I have in here are on the basis of things that I have already seen that we have that just need to be dusted off and sharpened, tools we have we have used in the past, ways in which we can improve on what already exists.

But going back to the overarching theme of putting Iran "on notice," I think that former National Security Adviser Flynn did the right thing. I think there needs to be follow-up in that regard, follow-up on what the new rules of engagement are, follow-up in terms of making very clear to the Iranians that escalation, we have a very clear intent of reestablishing escalation dominance, of changing the nature of the dynamics between the U.S. and Iranians and the Gulf in other places and Yemen as well.

But I also don't think that we have done nearly enough to point out the fact that while the original hostage crisis was in 1979, there is another hostage crisis. The Iranian regime continues to take Iranian-Americans and Canadian-Americans and other hyphenated Iranians hostage. It has become the systematic policy for the IRGC and for those businesses, particularly foreign businesses that are looking to get back into Iran, I think that needs to be part of, I guess, an overhaul of our media offensive and making clear about the dangers and risks not only to reputation, but literal risks of doing business in Iran.

So I think Iran needs to be put on notice on various other dimensions. The other thing I would say is know your customer and do due diligence. My understanding from foreign businesses, large multinationals that are going into Iran, is that those requirements are actually rather easy to satisfy. I think this committee might consider ways of enhancing those, making those stricter, raising the bar for companies that are looking to get back in.

The IRGC has done a very good job of cloaking itself, you know, two or three degrees removed from the core so that businesses, you know, can avoid that type of risk. But I think that they are ensconced in ways that ordinary businesses don't know and they are not being held liable to actually verify.

Corruption, I think, is the one thing that gets at the heart of all the Iranians. To the extent that you are going to move Iranians, channel that anger and get them to do more inside and outside of Iran to stand up and protest, I really think that we need to do a much better job of systematically pointing out how deep corruption is. And I think that there are certain ways of doing that not only by overhauling what I said, the Voice of America and Radio Free Europe, and actually returning to the day when those were tools that were part of U.S.-Iran policy, but also on U.S. Government Web sites I think that there needs to be putting businesses on notice as well.

I also think partners, proxies, and allies of the Iranian Government as well need to be put on notice and there are a lot of ways in which we can do that, and Chairman Royce mentioned some of those in some of the war zones in which we are all familiar. I look forward to expanding on some of these ideas, most of which I have mentioned in my testimony. Thank you.

[The prepared statement of Mr. Modell follows:]

"Iran on Notice: The Future of U.S. Policy Toward Iran"

Prepared testimony of Scott Modell
Managing Director, The Rapidan Group
Before the House of Representatives Committee on Foreign Affairs

February 16, 2017

Chairmen Royce, Ranking Member Engel, Members of the Committee, thank you for the opportunity to testify today. The election of Donald Trump and the apparent willingness of his national security team to sharpen U.S. policy toward Iran allow us to consider hard-hitting policy recommendations that were anathema to President Obama's softer, more conciliatory approach during the past eight years. A tougher approach should target the decayed base of popular support for the regime, ratchet up international law enforcement efforts, take advantage of increasingly intractable problems within the regime itself, and the lay the foundation for a multi-year effort to change the behavior of the regime. Despite all of its shortcomings and failings, however, the Islamic Republic is not on the verge of collapse. In the graphic below, the conditions for a "Persian spring" or even major reform are not present:

The Evolution of Change Indicators in Iran				
Leading indicators of change	Dec 1979	May 1996	May 2009	Feb 2017
Regime no longer functional	Yes	Somewhat	Somewhat	Somewhat
Economic downturn	Yes	Yes	Yes	Yes
Security services undermined	No	No	No	No
Political elite infighting	Yes	Somewhat	Somewhat	Somewhat
Elite support to opposition	No	No	Somewhat	No
Widespread popular dissatisfaction	Yes	Yes	Yes	Yes
Willingness to protest	Yes	No	Yes	No
Organized resistance	Yes	No	Yes	No
Charismatic leader	Yes	No	Somewhat	No
Tools to effectively communicate	Yes	No	Somewhat	Yes
	Why Khomeini won then			and why change is unlikely

Instead, the recommendations below argue for increasing military and non-military pressure to moderate regime behavior over time. If implemented, they would add some heft to the decision by former National Security Advisor Flynn to put Iran on notice, strengthen our own national security apparatus in the process, and send a clear signal that we intend to hold Iran accountable for its illicit and destabilizing activities.

Recommendation #1: Overhaul Voice of America (VOA) and Radio Free Europe (RFE)'s "Radio Farda." Ratings have hit rock bottom due to watered down programming, low morale, and the corrosive and undermining presence of regime apologists who often do a better job justifying Iran's nuclear program than the regime itself. There is no excuse for this, especially given the low credibility of government controlled media. A revitalized Persian media offensive has a target rich, anti-regime Iranian audience: 50 million regular viewers of satellite TV, 44 million internet users, 20 million users of social networks and "secure" messaging apps, and 18 million smart phones (all mostly used by youth). Suggested reforms include the following:

- In addition to programmatic changes, VOA and RFE should have a strict policy of employee screening. Existing background checks are inadequate, even on Iranians coming directly from IRIB and other Iranian govt. ministries. It would be fairly easy for a sophisticated intelligence service such as Iran's MOIS to infiltrate VOA and RFE and take the edge off of anti-regime programming.
- Deeply integrate VOA and RFE with U.S. Iran policy. VOA and RFE should go beyond reporting the news. They should also be platforms for explaining U.S. policy, exploiting divisions and conflicts within the regime, bolstering reformists and calling for free and fair elections, weakening international support for Iran, and highlighting Iran's links to regional destabilization. VOA should create a "Window to Washington" program on U.S. policy.
- Compound the impact of existing fissures in Iran: While the Green Movement is either dead or on life support, protests do occur on a very regular basis across the country. Persian media outlets should be shining a light on protestors, from angry factory workers and ethnic groups to women's rights activists and impoverished teachers. Even though these protests tend to be local and short-lived, we should help these "unconnected clusters of dissent" coalesce and lead to stronger anti-regime behavior. Congress should mandate regular reports from the Administration on the foreign policy value of U.S.-sponsored Persian media programs.
- Countering regime efforts to block transmissions: Congress should ensure VOA, RFE, and others have the capability to broadcast even when the regime blocks incoming transmission. This could include the use of wireless signals (WIMAX) into areas such as Iranian Kurdistan where the govt. regularly blocks foreign media signals. Our allies in the region have potential roles to play in this regard.
- Include programs that expose the interconnectivity between the IRGC's existing economic empire and corruption. Investigations into the illicit networks of Reza Zarrab and Babak Zanjani alone could fill dozens of hours of air time. VOA and RFE should amplify their reporting on corruption by building on the work of popular shows such as the Last Page ("Safhe-ye Akhar").

Recommendation #2: Use the reforms to Persian media mentioned above to spearhead an information warfare campaign against Iran. In addition to highlighting ties to terrorism and corruption, U.S.-led efforts should focus on harnessing the untapped anger, resentment, and willingness to speak out against the regime.

- Women: The women's movement in Iran is more about recapturing the rights women used to have. Nobel Laureate, Shirin Ebadi, was a judge before the 1979 Islamic Revolution. Today, women are prohibited by law from becoming judges. No social group has lost as much as women in the Islamic Republic, and no issue packs more hidden energy in Iran than women's rights and gender equality.

- Teachers and other low wage earners: The regime's inability to counter growing inequality and poverty is a growing problem. Efforts have failed and the regime has no plan for lifting the growing mass of low wage earners above the poverty line. The results is evident in some sort of strike or demonstration almost every day in Iran.
- Ethnic Groups: Several are so disenfranchised in the Islamic Republic that they are not allowed to name their children in their native languages. The regime has prevented the construction of a Sunni mosque in Tehran, despite the more than one million Sunni residents. The plight of Azeri, Baluch, and other ethnic minorities are important axes of Iran's dysfunctional civil society.
- Social Crises: The regime's malfeasance has created a number of crises in areas from health to welfare, each of which has spurred the creation of small but organized movements. Record levels of air pollution in Tehran and other major cities, harmful radiation due to government interference with satellite TV signals, high youth unemployment, drug addiction, and rampant prostitution.

Recommendation #3: Declassify intelligence that shows the links between Iran, al-Qa'ida, the Taliban, and violent Sunni and Shia terrorist groups. Iran has successfully hijacked the "global war on terror" narrative that used to be led by the United States. Today, it effectively markets itself as the leading state sponsor of counter-terrorism. This exposure should extend to the drug trade.

- Links between al-Qa'ida and Iran's security services exist and should be exploited as part of the media campaign mentioned above. It would undermine Iran's self-proclaimed status on the front lines of the war against radical Islam, while further eroding domestic support for the last generation's revolutionary zeal.
- This should go hand in hand with releases of similar information on GCC support to Sunni extremists. US credibility will benefit most if we air the dirty laundry of all sides. Deputy Crown Prince Mohamed bin Salman (MbS) and his generation could become effective partners in this regard as they attempt to rebrand the Kingdom.
- Iran's hand in drug trafficking, both inside Iran and across the region, should be further explored and exploited. Several international narcotics trafficking investigations have pointed to IRGC involvement, either in distribution inside Iran or in transit on the way to Turkey and ultimately Europe and the United States.

Recommendation #4: Expand and facilitate the PL-110 program. There are few incentives for well-placed individuals inside the Iranian government to risk their lives to cooperate with the U.S. government. Congress should broaden PL-110 authorities to increase the number of aliens U.S. government agencies can bring into the United States every year. The process is lengthy, cumbersome, and overly restrictive.

- D/CIA has the right to give away 100 green cards every year to individuals who provide extraordinary assistance to U.S. intelligence collection and covert action efforts. This number should increase dramatically in order to increase the number of potential defectors and to stimulate the "brain drain" of Iranian scientists and senior technocrats from government agencies overseeing Iran's most sensitive nuclear and conventional military sites, ongoing R&D, strategic policy, and illicit procurement. We should encourage our European counterparts to do the same.

- PL-110 should not be limited to intelligence activities. We should also reward those who enable international law enforcement efforts. Investigations and operations that lead to the identification, arrest, and even extradition of individuals involved in activities that violate the JCPOA, support terrorist proxies, etc.
- An expansion of PL-110 could go hand in hand with a reinvigorated Treasury attache cadre in areas around the world that are vulnerable to transnational organized crime. Sanctions, designations, and other Treasury actions from Washington can only go so far. Our overseas national security and diplomatic corps has a very limited understanding of threat finance, stunting the development of working-level law enforcement relationships.

Recommendation #5: Expose the scope of Iranian corruption and human rights abuse by adding Iranian individuals to the Magnitsky List, or by creating one specific to Iran. Most Iranians are well aware of the staggering depth of corruption in Iran today, particularly among the IRGC and conservative power elite. Even President Rouhani routinely regards corruption as one of the largest failures of the Islamic Revolution.

- Congress should pass legislation calling on the Administration to produce quarterly reports on Iranian government corruption and violations of human rights. The unclassified report would further delegitimize Iran's ruling class, enable democratic and reform-minded elites in Iran, serve as fodder for English and Persian media, and underscore U.S. support to the silent majority of Iranians who are increasingly disconnected to the Islamic Revolution.
- Congress should also provide funding for U.S. government website upgrades. Efforts to denigrate the regime would be well served if our own law enforcement websites had the capacity to serve as secure transceivers of valuable information. Doing so would occasionally uncover compromising information that could be exploited in social media, used in law enforcement investigations, or disseminated to companies that are either active in Iran or considering the possibility.
- Crime matrix: Treasury or State should have a website with a matrix that lists individuals and entities in Iran followed by their involvement in or links to corruption, human rights violations, terrorism, money laundering, drug trafficking, nuclear proliferation, etc. The worst offenders of the regime should be highlighted up front, from the Supreme Leader himself and his closest financial managers such as Vahid Haqqanian and Mohammad Mokhber to the head of finance for the Astan-e Qods Foundation, Sayyed Morteza Bakhtiari.

Recommendation #6: Bolster Najaf, Iran's main rival in the competition for leadership over the worldwide Shia community. Najaf in Iraq and Qom in Iran have long struggled to be the primary "source of emulation" for Shiites around the world. Iran's model is a theocracy that puts the clergy in positions of political power, whereas Iraq's leading authority Grand Ayatollah Sistani sticks to a more orthodox interpretation of Shia Islam that encourages the clergy to steer clear of politics.

- We should encourage Arab allies to openly support Najaf's more tolerant "quietist" traditions, particularly important in the run-up to a possible succession of Supreme Leader Khamenei in Iran and the passing on of the 86 year-old Sistani.
- This should involve the promotion of the most prominent and revered figures in Iran such as Ayatollah Shirazi and others (who are against Khamenei) and in Iraq who support more

tolerant and less militant and politicized forms of Shia Islam. Iran is aggressively involved in a soft war to undermine support for Sistani and other Grand Ayatollahs likely to replace him.

Recommendation #7: Change the rules of engagement. IRGC fast boats swarming U.S. vessels is one dimension of a sustained pattern of provocation in the Gulf. There were at least 35 such "close encounters" in 2016 alone, a constant reminder of Iran's threat to commercial traffic carrying 17 million barrels per day of oil and gas through the Strait of Hormuz.

- The U.S. should deal militarily with IRGC threats and harassment in the Gulf. Tough rhetoric and firing warning shots are not enough to deter Iranian aggression. New rules of engagement should be made clear to Iran in keeping with General Flynn's marker to put Iran on notice.
- U.S. should provide missile defense, security guarantees, and overt training and support to Bahrain and our GCC allies to deter and defend against the full spectrum of asymmetric threats posed by Iran.
- The U.S. should also encourage Saudi Arabia and its GCC partners to continue their regional strategy of pushing back against Iranian aggression across the region. As Riyadh in particular has learned in Syria and Yemen, there is a steep learning curve that will last for several years. On the other hand, Iran has been active in cyber war, proxy war, conventional war, and various forms of covert action for decades. If we ever hope to downsize our role, the GCC countries must do more to balance security in the region.

These are just a few recommendations for a new U.S. policy on Iran that focuses more intently on Iran's malign, destabilizing behavior across the region. I appreciate the opportunity to present them before the Committee.

STATEMENT OF ANDREW EXUM, PH.D., CONTRIBUTING EDITOR, THE ATLANTIC

Mr. EXUM. Mr. Chairman and Mr. Ranking Member, thank you so much for the opportunity to speak to the committee today. I have been asked to present testimony on Iran and I will do so in my capacity as the former Deputy Assistant Secretary of Defense for Middle East Policy during the Obama administration. I left the Department of Defense last month and my testimony today was cleared by the Department to ensure what I tell you remains at the appropriate level of classification and is as boring as possible for the rest of you listening in, but I will do my best to talk about things within the constraints I have been given.

The United States has three vital interests in the Middle East: The security of the State of Israel, countering terrorism and the proliferation of weapons of mass destruction, and freedom of navigation and commerce in and around the Arabian Peninsula which all of you know is the home to vast hydrocarbon reserves. Iran can and does pose a threat to all of those interests and it does so in three ways: Its nuclear program, its buildup of conventional arms, and what we call its asymmetric activities that support the proxies such as Hezbollah or some of the Shia militias in Iraq.

During the Obama administration we countered Iran through what we called our four Ps: Our posture, our plans, our partners, and our preparedness. With respect to posture, we have about 35,000 troops in and around the Persian Gulf alone. We have major airbases in Kuwait, Qatar, and the UAE. We have a major naval base in Bahrain. And these bases and the troops operating out of them allow us to ensure freedom of navigation in and around the Arabian Peninsula, combat terror groups—for many of these forces are in the skies above Iraq and Syria right now—and deter conventional Iranian aggression against our Gulf partners.

We maintain a robust suite of plans to respond to regional contingencies. In my capacity at the Pentagon I reviewed these plans. They are real, they are resourced, and our forces are ready to execute them. Over the past three decades, meanwhile, we have invested in our regional partnerships, specifically building partnership capacity in our Gulf partners.

We have a long way to go, but one of the areas where we have made the most progress, ballistic missile defense, helps us counter Iran's build-up of conventional weapons. We also engaged in unprecedented levels of defense and intelligence cooperation with Israel while making available some of our most advanced U.S.-made weapons to Gulf partners.

Finally, we have our preparedness, and we chose this word because we needed the fourth P for people like me to remember. But what this really stands for, the many dozens of bilateral, unilateral, multilateral exercises we conduct on an annual basis to help us prepare for regional contingencies.

So how are we doing? I will be blunt in my assessment and then offer some words of advice for this new administration as well as some words of caution for this committee. Specifically, I will argue that this administration's strategic flirtation with Russia is incompatible with what I assess to be its desire to pressure and counter Iran.

First, the Department of Defense did not play a role in negotiating the nuclear deal with Iran, but the deal very much helped the U.S. military. Despite all the sturm and drang here in Washington and elsewhere in the summer of 2015, most strategic planners I have spoken with both here and in the region see the deal as offering real, positive opportunities both for the United States and for Iran.

As you know, the Pentagon was always in charge of providing the enforcement mechanism for U.S. policy. If Iran cheats we will know about it, and the Pentagon is prepared to act accordingly. From our perspective then the nuclear deal was a pretty good deal because it constrained Iran while placing no such constraints on us.

Iran also has some opportunities of course, and it appears to be largely squandering them. Some optimists in the Obama administration had hoped the nuclear negotiations would be a way to bring Iran in from the cold, so to speak, and encourage Iran to play a more helpful role regionally. The view of these optimists was not universally shared within the administration.

Many of us argued within the administration and to our allies that the reason we needed to sign a deal with Iran was not because Iran is a benign actor but because they are a malign actor and thus needed to be prevented from acquiring a nuclear weapon. Iran's actions since signing the nuclear deal have vindicated the pessimists. Iran continues a robust build-up of conventional weapons, including what we military folks call anti-access, area denial weapons like anti-ship cruise missiles and air defense systems, and while I don't think our own military commanders are losing sleep over these weapons just yet, I know our regional partners are.

And here is my first word of caution. These weapons systems for the most part are not indigenous to the Islamic Republic of Iran. These are Russian weapons, sold by Russia to Iran with the aim of constraining U.S. freedom of maneuver in strategically important waterways and airways. Any serious effort to counter the build-up of these Iranian capabilities has to take Russia into account.

Iran is also continuing what I would call its asymmetric activities. Its support to Shia and allied militia in Lebanon, Iraq, Syria, and Yemen continues. The presence of anti-ship cruise missiles in Yemen is especially concerning since it threatens a key commercial waterway, the Bab al-Mandeb.

And let me be blunt again regarding the administration's overtures to Russia. In Syria it will be exceptionally difficult and likely impossible to reach any accommodation with Russia and the regime in Damascus that does not end up strengthening Iran and its proxies, including Hezbollah. So before the administration goes down that path they should recognize that in the short term at least they are going to embolden some of the very people they have pledged to counter in the region. And they will embolden Iran and these groups to the detriment of Israel's security.

In Iraq, meanwhile, the Islamic State is on a clear path to defeat. But the long term threat to Iraq's sovereignty is both Kurdish separatism and the Shia militia, many of them supported by Iran, that exist only loosely affiliated with the Iraqi state. In addition, Iraq's long term stability will be dependent on the United States being able to keep a small contingent of trainers and special operators in the country, which is why the President's dismissive comments about the Iraqi Government, his comments about how we should have taken Iraq's oil, and his ban on Iraqis coming to the United States have been so strategically misguided.

This all plays into a narrative of an Iran that very much views Iraq as a zero-sum game with the United States. It has spent millions of dollars to convince Iraqis that we have the types of malign activities toward Iraq that the President seems to in fact have but which few other share. If the United States wants to push back on that it needs to do so in the President's words and with robust diplomacy.

I would also caution this administration from trying to push back against Iran and its proxies in Iraq right now. We have a Sunni terrorist enemy to defeat in Iraq and our 5,000 soldiers in Iraq need to focus on them not on war with Iran's proxies. I fought in Iraq, and as any of you who fought there remember, Iran can make our life pretty miserable. So we don't need that fight right now and we should sequence how we push back on them.

Finally, a few words on Yemen. We have talked about Islamic fundamentalism, but I am somewhat of a freedom of navigation fundamentalist. The United States should be prepared to robustly counter any threats to key waterways, and I am not going to lose any sleep if a couple of Houthis die because they made an error of firing an anti-ship cruise missile into the Bab al-Mandeb.

I should note though that the vast, vast majority of commercial traffic—1,400 vessels, 80 million tons on a monthly basis—that flows through the Bab al-Mandeb is not American. It comes from the European Union, India, China, Korea; these are the countries that have the most at stake in any actions which threatens shipping, and before the administration escalates a war in Yemen it should start with some multilateral diplomacy telling Iran, in essence, to knock it off, lest their own commercial interests be at stake.

In conclusion, in Secretary Mattis we have a Secretary of Defense who keenly understands the threat posed by Iran. And in Secretary Tillerson and Gary Cohn we have, respectively, a Secretary of State and a director of the Economic Council who understand the centrality of market access to hydrocarbon resources in the Gulf to the global economy.

So there is some cause for optimism that this administration will eventually put together a coherent strategy to counter Iran's malign activities in a way that serves U.S. interests. But the contradictions in the administration's strategic initiatives thus far, not to mention the alarming and unprecedented dysfunction within the national security decision making process, leave plenty of room for worry as well.

Mr. Chairman, thank you for allowing me to go over.

[The prepared statement of Mr. Exum follows:]

DR. ANDREW EXUM

TESTIMONY BEFORE THE FOREIGN AFFAIRS COMMITTEE

(1604 WORDS, 5 MINUTES)

Mr. Chairman, Mr. Ranking Member, thank you so much for the opportunity to speak to the committee today.

I've been asked to present testimony on Iran, and I'll do so in my capacity as the former deputy assistant secretary of defense for Middle East policy in the Obama Administration. I left the Department of Defense last month, and my testimony today was cleared by the Department to ensure what I tell you remains at the appropriate level of classification. I don't need to remind any of you, though, that restricting our discussion to the unclassified level constrains what I can say about the way in which the Obama Administration addressed the challenges posed by Iran.

The United States has three vital interests in the Middle East: the security of the state of Israel, countering terrorism and the proliferation of weapons of mass destruction, and freedom of navigation and commerce in and around the Arabian Peninsula, which as you all know is home to vast hydrocarbon reserves.

Iran can and does pose a threat to all of those interests, and it does so in three ways: its nuclear program, its build-up of conventional arms, and what we call its asymmetric activities – its support to proxies such as Hizballah or some of the Shia militias in Iraq.

During the Obama Administration, we countered Iran through what we called our four Ps: our posture, our plans, our partners, and our preparedness.

With respect to our posture, we have about 35,000 troops in and around the Persian Gulf alone. We have major air bases in Kuwait, Qatar, and the United Arab Emirates. We have a major naval base in Bahrain. These bases and the troops operating out of them allow us to both ensure freedom of navigation in and around the Arabian Peninsula, combat terror groups – for many of these troops are currently busy in the skies over Iraq and Syria – and deter conventional Iranian aggression against our Gulf partners.

We maintain a robust suite of plans to respond to regional contingencies. In my capacity at the Department of Defense, I reviewed these plans. They are real, they are resourced, and our forces are ready to execute them.

Over the past three decades, meanwhile, we have invested in our regional partnerships, and specifically, building capacity in our Gulf partners. We have a long way to go, but one of the areas where we have made the most progress – ballistic missile defense – helps us counter Iran's build-up of conventional weapons. We also engaged in unprecedented levels of defense and intelligence cooperation with Israel while making available some of our most advanced U.S.-made weapons to Gulf partners.

Finally, we have our preparedness. We chose this word because we needed a fourth "p," frankly, but what this really stands for is the many dozens of unilateral, bilateral, and multilateral exercises we conduct on an annual basis to help us prepare for regional contingencies.

So how are we doing? I'll be blunt in my assessment and then offer some words of advice for this new administration as well as some words of caution for this committee. Specifically, I will argue that this administration's strategic flirtation with Russia is incompatible with what I assess to be its desire to pressure and counter Iran.

First, the Department of Defense did not play a role in negotiating the nuclear deal with Iran, but the deal very much helps the U.S. military. Despite all the *sturm und drang* here in Washington and elsewhere in the summer of 2015, most strategic planners with whom I have spoken – both here and in the region – see the deal as offering real, positive opportunities to both the United States and Iran.

As you know, the Department of Defense was always in charge of providing the enforcement mechanism for U.S. policy. If Iran cheats, we will know about it, and the Department of Defense is prepared to act accordingly. From our perspective, then, the nuclear deal was a pretty good deal because it constrained Iran while placing no such constraints on us.

Iran also has some opportunities, of course, and it appears to be largely squandering them. Some optimists in the Obama Administration had hoped the nuclear negotiations would be a way to bring Iran in from the cold, so to speak, and encourage Iran to play a more helpful role regionally. The view of these optimists was not universally shared within the administration: many of us argued within the administration and to our allies that the reason we needed to sign this deal with Iran was not because Iran is a benign actor but because it is a malign actor – and thus needed to be prevented from acquiring nuclear weapons. Iran's actions since signing the nuclear deal have somewhat vindicated us pessimists.

Iran continues a robust build-up of conventional weapons – including what we military folks would call anti-access, area denial weapons like anti-ship cruise missiles and air defense systems. I don't think our military commanders are losing sleep over these weapons systems just yet, but I know our regional partners are. Here's my first word of caution: these weapons systems, for the most part, are not indigenous to the Islamic Republic of Iran. These are Russian weapons, sold by Russia to Iran, with the aim of constraining U.S. freedom of maneuver in strategically important waterways and airways. Any serious effort to counter the build-up of these Iranian capabilities, then, has to take Russia into account.

Iran is also continuing what I will call its asymmetric activities. Its support to Shia and allied militia in Lebanon, Iraq, Syria, and Yemen continues. The presence of anti-ship cruise missiles into Yemen is especially concerning since it threatens a key commercial waterway, the Bab al-Mandeb.

Let me be blunt again regarding the administration's overtures to Russia: in Syria, it will be exceptionally difficult and likely impossible to reach any kind of accommodation with Russia and the regime in Damascus that does not end up strengthening Iran and its proxies, including Hizballah. So before the administration goes down that path, they should recognize that in the short term at least, they are going to embolden some of the very people they have pledged to counter in the region. And they will embolden Iran and these groups to the detriment of Israel's security.

In Iraq, meanwhile, the Islamic State is on a clear path to defeat. But the long-term threat to Iraq's sovereignty is both Kurdish separatism and the Shia militias – many of them supported by Iran – that exist only loosely affiliated with the Iraqi state. In addition, Iraq's long-term stability will be dependent on the United States being able to keep a small contingent of trainers and special operators in the country – which is why the president's dismissive comments about the Iraqi government, his comments about how we should have taken Iraq's oil, and his ban on Iraqis coming to the United

States have been so strategically misguided. This all plays into the narrative of an Iran that very much views Iraq as a zero-sum game with the United States and has spent millions of dollars to convince Iraqis that we have the kind of malign attitudes toward Iraq that the president seems to, in fact, actually have but which few others share. If the United States wants to push back on that, it needs to do so in the president's words and with robust diplomacy. I would caution the administration from trying to push back on Iran or its proxies militarily in Iraq – at least for now. We still have a Sunni terrorist enemy to defeat in Iraq, and our 5,000 troops in Iraq need to focus on the fight against the Islamic State, not war with Iran's proxies. I fought in Iraq, and any of us who served there remember the ways in which Iran can make life miserable for U.S. troops there. We don't need that fight right now.

Finally, a few words on Yemen. We've talked about Islamic fundamentalism, but I'm somewhat of a freedom of navigation fundamentalist: the United States should be prepared to robustly counter any threats to key waterways, and I'm not going to lose any sleep if a couple of Houthis die because they made the error of firing an anti-ship cruise missile into the Bab al-Mandeb. I should note, though, that the vast, vast majority of commercial traffic – roughly 1,400 vessels, or 80 million tons – that flows

through the Bab al-Mandeb on a monthly basis is not American: it is from

the European Union, India, China, and Korea. Those are the countries that

have the most at stake in any actions which threaten shipping through the

Bab al-Mandeb, and before the administration escalates a war in Yemen, it

should start with some multilateral diplomacy telling Iran, in essence, to

knock it off lest its own commercial interests fall under threat.

In Secretary Mattis, we have a Secretary of Defense who keenly understands

the threat posed by Iran. And in Secretary Tillerson and Gary Cohn, we

have, respectively, a Secretary of State and a Director of the Economic

Council who understand the centrality of market access to hydrocarbon

resources in the Gulf to the global economy.

So there's some cause for optimism that this administration will eventually

put together a coherent strategy to counter Iran's malign activities in a way

that serves U.S. interests. But the contradictions in the administration's

strategic initiatives thus far, not to mention the alarming dysfunction within

the national security decision-making process, leave plenty of room for

worry as well.

———

Chairman ROYCE. Thank you, Mr. Exum. Thank you to the panel. One of the questions that I was going to direct at Mr. Albright concerned a portion of your testimony where you said that the previous administration interfered in U.S. law enforcement efforts when it came to them blocking the efforts to arrest and convict Iranians and their agents engaged in breaking U.S. export and sanctions laws.

One of the focuses I have is sort of reversing that policy, especially with respect to the IRGC, but what measures can we take to send the signal that extraditing and arresting and convicting those that are involved in breaking our laws has to be a priority? Mr.

ALBRIGHT. Well, first thing, I think some of these memos and extradition requests should be revisited. I mean they still exist, some cases may still be active. I mean these are not public cases.

The other, and I must say one of the impacts that I heard very clearly was that this in a sense interfering in what the investigators were doing in our enforcement agencies was discouraging, and these are hard cases to launch and they hesitate to do more.

So I think the administration should send a very strong signal that it fully supports these investigations and prosecutions of these Iranian and Iranian agents.

Chairman ROYCE. So that would have to be through State and so it was the State Department——

Mr. ALBRIGHT. That is right.

Chairman ROYCE [continuing]. That put the kibosh on it.

Mr. ALBRIGHT. Well, that is where they tended to die.

Chairman ROYCE. Yes.

Mr. ALBRIGHT. So that is where they tended to die, but I think it has to be done at the White House level.

Chairman ROYCE. Okay.

Mr. ALBRIGHT. And to get these cases moving again, because I think my understanding is Iran hasn't stopped its illicit activities and it is very important to counter them.

Chairman ROYCE. Well, another way to counter it, and I will go to Ms. Bauer's comment here, but I bet there would be a tremendous ripple effect from sanctioning just one or two European companies for transactions with the Iranian Revolutionary Guard Corps. They are the main economic player in Iran.

And I think you had a line in your testimony where you said that the application of U.S. secondary sanctions for dealing with the Iranian Revolutionary Guard Corps remains a significant risk for companies looking to reengage with Iran and that this application of secondary sanctions has never been done.

So another question is why not and what would the impact be if our response now to their missile tests and maybe to General Soleimani's trip 2 days ago to Moscow is such a robust action? And let's push that button there.

Ms. BAUER. Thank you, Chairman. Indeed, the remaining sanctions on the IRGC and the fact that they include secondary sanctions risks remains a great deterrent to businesses looking to reengage with Iran. And in fact that is one reason I think why you haven't seen action against a European country in particular is that they do not want to lose access to the U.S. financial system, and so they are able to look at the OFAC list and ensure that they don't do business with anyone on that list or anyone who holds a 50 percent or an aggregated 50 percent share of a business they are working with.

So they are able to do some due diligence. Where they are not confident with the due diligence it appears that they are not engaging. But there are things that could be done to make it harder and to isolate the IRGC further, for example, designating additional IRGC affiliates to make it clear to those companies going in.

Chairman ROYCE. So maybe those with less than a 50 percent ownership share but you could expand that out, or you are saying there is affiliates out there that we haven't captured yet?

Ms. BAUER. There are affiliates who haven't been listed. Even those that are not listed by operation of law, companies are restricted or could be sanctioned for doing business.

Chairman ROYCE. Why don't we do this on that answer. Why don't I just ask the panel if you have ideas on that, if you could give me some specifics, and I could just get to this Soleimani question which I wanted to ask, because it was a surprise to me, you know, to see him travel again to Moscow. This is the third time he has done it, and as a matter of fact he is there right now. And I would just ask the panel for any creative solutions for effectively pushing back on his continued travel.

And the thing I find most objectionable here is that he has been, you know, fingered as the fellow behind the death of many Americans, the one who plotted the Russian-Iranian tag team slaughter that went on in Syria in the middle of the Iranian negotiations. I mean there have been so much that this guy, as head of the Qud Forces—which is in charge of assassinations outside the country—has been responsible for, attacks across Europe and so forth where they take out anybody perceived to be an enemy of the regime.

I mean this is a really bloodthirsty guy. And it seems to me that the reason he is headed to Moscow for these meetings has got to be the ballistic missile systems or other weapons systems that he intends to introduce into the theater. So ideas on how to react to that? Maybe Mr. Modell, do you have a——

Mr. MODELL. One of the things that I have thought and again what I hear from Iranians all the time is why is the U.S. Government not doing more to come up with a large matrix of all IRGC officials that we know of, businesses that we know that are linked, and publicize it constantly and to show their links to corruption? I mean this isn't necessarily going to directly address the Soleimani issue, but I think it is going to significantly weaken the IRGC.

So when you are talking about publicizing the——

Chairman ROYCE. Well, I think this cuts into another point you made in your testimony here about the need to make some changes of the broadcasting into Iran so that yes, it is objective but we do touch on issues that is important there. We now have a single head of the agency who has the ability to direct information.

And so as information spills out about corruption or whatever that access to that information on social media and on a platform of radio and television should be available so that people know exactly what has happened here with respect to the IRGC taking all of these assets usually through nationalization and transferring them to the ownership of the Revolutionary Guard Corps.

I need to go to Mr. Engel. My time has expired. Thank you very much, panel.

Mr. ENGEL. Thank you, Mr. Chairman. Dr. Exum, let me ask you this. In your testimony you pointed out one way in which Russia and Iran collaborate to destabilize the Middle East. You mentioned that Russia provides Iran with anti-access, area denial weapons like anti-ship cruise missiles and air defense systems. Obviously this is very disconcerting to us and our allies because their goal is using these weapons to inhibit freedom of movement in strategic waterways and airways.

There have been Russian media reports that Iran and Russia are in discussions over $10 billion in weapons. How would you suggest the Trump administration respond to this?

Mr. EXUM. Well, I think one of the things that the Trump administration can do and then here with respect to sanctions that defer to the sanctions experts, because I am sure that there are aspects outside of the military lane that you can use. I think with respect to diplomacy, I will just focus on diplomacy and the military steps that I think he can take with respect to diplomacy by constraining the access to waterways.

And look, these are, we don't need the oil and gas that is coming out the Persian Gulf as much as the global markets need them and as much as we need them for the stability of the global economy. So it is not just the United States or the Trump administration that has a stake in this, that has a stake in freedom of navigation and freedom of commerce in and around the Arabian Peninsula. I would think that you would start with a large multilateral effort to pressure Iran on the deployment of these weapons systems and on Russia on the sales of these weapons systems.

From a military perspective we are already doing quite a lot. Again I don't think that the commander of NAVCENT would argue that his freedom of movement is in any way constrained right now, but it is clear that we need to do two things. We need to increase the degree to which we have ballistic and air missile, or integrated air and missile defense systems, within the Middle East. That includes both sales to partners and increasing partner capacity, but it also means that our partners in the region need to get more serious about their own maritime capabilities. Historically, maritime capability of the Navy has been the third of three services within most of our Gulf militaries. They need to get serious about their own efforts to be able to keep the waterways in and around the Arabian Peninsula secure.

And I would defer again, like I said, to my Treasury colleagues or my colleagues from the Washington Institute with respect to what more we can do in terms of sanctioning those Russian businesses or those Iranians that are purchasing these types of weapons systems, Mr. Ranking Member.

Mr. ENGEL. Thank you. Anybody else have comments on that?

Mr. MODELL. Mr. Ranking Member, the only thing I would say is that it is a very asymmetric process that Iran is involved in and that includes commercial acquisition of the conventional military stuff. Building on what Dr. Exum is saying, I think we have not done enough to work with our allies in the region, particularly in the GCC which is often the site of enabling Iran to do these things, to front companies based in their own Emirates, for instance, to develop the capabilities to work asymmetrically in a defensive capacity. And I don't think we are systematically oriented in that sense.

Mr. ENGEL. Thank you.

Mr. Albright, let me ask you this. You have criticized the IAEA for lack of transparency in reporting and I quote you, this is what you said: "The IAEA reporting continues to lack critical technical details that implementation of the agreement. Its lack of information in the IAEA reports combined with the secrecy surrounding the decision making of the Joint Commission is a serious shortcoming on the implementation of the JCPOA and erodes support for this important deal."

Let me ask you this, what information is missing from IAEA reporting and what information do you need to be made public? What specific recommendations do you have for the Trump administration and Congress to encourage more transparency so that experts like you can better evaluate the implementation?

Mr. ALBRIGHT. Well, in my testimony I gave there is a footnote and I apologize for making a footnote. But essentially the IAEA is not reporting on almost any of the technical details that it used to report on—levels of enriched uranium, controversies with Iran. I mean Iran is pushing limits of the JCPOA. The IAEA may or may not be pushing back but it could report on the status of that. So I would say that they are providing very little information.

On heavy water we hear a lot, well, they are over, you know, the cap of 130 tons by 100 kilograms, they leave out 70 tons was sent off to Oman in a kind of a clever trick that in essence allowed Iran to be 70 tons over the cap on heavy water, if you judge that cap by the heavy water Iran owns and controls.

So I think that there is a lack of information inhibiting analysis, and the lack of information is providing a false narrative about where things are at and we need a lot more information. Now I will say under pressure, some from Congress, some from us, some from the media, the Joint Commission did decide in December to start releasing its major decisions publicly. I mean I don't think they wanted to do that but I think that they felt the absolute need to do it. And so I think pressure does work in this case and I think the Trump administration should push for much more openness.

Mr. ENGEL. Thank you, Mr. Chairman, my time is up. Thank you.

Chairman ROYCE. Thank you, Mr. Engel. We go to Mr. Rohrabacher of California.

Mr. ROHRABACHER. Thank you, Mr. Chairman. And I would like to thank you and the ranking member for again providing us the information and a focus on a very significant element to our nation's security, and so thank you both. And I would identify myself certainly with your opening statement.

I am however, and this panel has not changed my, I don't know if it is observation or my analysis that frankly our policy toward Iran and the mullah regime in Iran has been detached from reality in that it is basically wishful thinking of the worst sort. Let me just mention about Russia and how they have armed the mullah regime, this horrible dictatorship, with weapons to shoot planes out of the air and take care of that type of military threat.

Quite frankly, we are not going to invade Iran. I don't see it even if they have a bomb we are not going to invade Iran. Those weapons are aimed at preventing some sort of, or countering a military threat to that regime which now has a positive relationship with Moscow. That if we are going to get rid of the mullah regime it won't be U.S. military personnel with U.S. weapons going in and doing that job.

If we are going to get rid, and unfortunately all the talk about that and all the details about every little increment in which the Iranian mullah regime now is closer to getting a bomb has taken us away from the real solution, the only solution which is make sure that we deal with the people of Iran who hate the mullahs. And you are taking focus away from that by talking about weapons systems and this.

We need to make, while we left the Baluch who would be in charge of the Strait of Hormuz I might add if we would support their fight against the mullah regime. The Kurds, there are more Kurds in Iran than there are in Iraq. The Azeris, we have Azerbaijan right next door that is willing to help. But all of this time, and even the Persian element were as ready to overthrow the mullahs several years ago in this Green Revolution and we let them go without any, even verbal, support for their effort.

Now getting rid of the mullah regime by helping the people of Iran is the answer. You have Persians, the MEK, I know as everybody criticizes them because they have a checkered past, well, they also, they have been willing to help us get rid of the mullah regime and they have been struggling for a more democratic government along with the other Persians who are there. Ninety percent of the Persians don't like it. And like you said as you would expect from a journalist to focus in on the corruption and the repression that is going on. Well, if we focus on that that is how we would mobilize the only real power we have to get rid of them which is the Iranian people themselves.

And one last note about this idea about all this focus on how much heavy water they have and et cetera, et cetera. We gave them $150 billion with this nonsensical treaty that we signed with them, $150 billion were made at their disposal. How much do you think it would cost them to buy a nuclear weapon from Pakistan? It wouldn't cost, I bet it wouldn't even cost $1 billion. I bet they could get it for in the tens of millions, if not $100 million. The fact is that regime with its hands on a military capability of nuclear weapons, that is the threat. It is the regime, it is not the weapon itself.

So I think we should quit focusing America's attention on things that will not change the situation and make us any safer. And again talking about how much heavy water they have and how are they going to be able to stop them from building their own bomb, if they want to bomb now they can afford to buy it. And the answer is the mullahs have got to go. The mullah regime has to leave and how we get rid of it is not through American military operations, but instead reaching out to the people of Iran and helping them win their freedom.

And that is, if anybody in the panel would like to spend their time refuting that, please go right ahead. How about my journalist friend, go right ahead.

Mr. EXUM. Well, sir, first off, thank you for that. I will be blunt. First off, you know, if it were to come to those types of activities, and then I well know your biography, I know your experience, you would know that the Department of Defense, this is not within our wheelhouse so to speak. You know, any outreach toward separatist movements is usually done either clandestinely or overtly through diplomatic channels. And there have, you know, certainly been examples where we have done that.

I think with respect to, I will focus on one thing which is the note about the dollars that Iran has. First off, you know, Iran always has the cash on hand if they wanted to, you know, purchase a nuclear weapon. I think—and I hate to do this, I am putting on my Ph.D. hat now—there is a lot of academic literature and a lot of analysis that would suggest that that is not a really likely thing. So if you were the Pakistanis and you sell a nuclear weapon to somebody, first off, you lose all of the control that you would have on that nuclear weapon and you would get all of the blowback if it is used. So I think that threat, although it is real and it is some thing that we carefully monitor, it is something that contains a lot of risk for anybody that would sell that.

The second thing I would say is that when it comes to money and what the Iranians are doing in terms of the asymmetric activities, in terms of these nefarious activities, a lot of these things are really cheap and they didn't need the money to keep doing this stuff. What they are doing in Yemen, what they are doing in Syria and Iraq, it is not that expensive to begin with.

And as we have established, if the Quds Force wants to get a piece of the budget they are going to get a piece of the budget. They are going to get their way and thus far they have gotten their way with respect to I guess what we would call the Islamic regime's discretionary spending. But, and I don't think that the amount of money that was freed up, which is a little less when you look at actually the liquid assets, has had much of an effect on what Qasem Soleimani and his lieutenants are doing in Iraq and Syria.

Chairman ROYCE. We go now to Mr. Brad Sherman of California.

Mr. SHERMAN. The gentleman from California, Mr. Royce, makes some interesting points and the chairman was quite indulgent with him on time. I hope that inspires a whole new approach.

Chairman ROYCE. Well, certainly with respect to Mr. Brad Sherman it does, so thank you.

Mr. SHERMAN. Because I do want to deal with some of the points he raises. But before I do that in some minds the picture of the Islamic Republic of Iran, this regime, is the smiling face of its foreign minister Javad Zarif—dapper, debonair—in Geneva. The real face of this regime, the real picture of this regime is Alan Kurdi, that 3 year-old boy on the beach in Turkey in the Mediterranean, one of 400,000 Syrians who died as a result of the Islamic Republic's support for the butcher in Damascus.

I for one don't think that we can excuse Russian arms sales to Iran on the theory that we are going to achieve regime change any time soon. We have watched the Arab Spring. We have seen which regimes survive and which don't. Those regimes that have 50,000 thugs willing to machine gun their own citizens survive. Those whose army is unwilling to do that and are confronted by their own people don't. And we have had other panels so I want to ask this panel, I have been assured by other panels that there are tens of thousands of Quds Force soldiers willing to machine gun other Iranians if that is what it takes to keep this regime in force.

The gentleman from California says that the weapons that Russia is selling they are only defensive, it wouldn't affect us. But of course the S300s are the anti-aircraft weapons that make it much more difficult for Israel or even the United States to take out this nuclear program if that becomes necessary, and the fact that all options are on the table is the only thing that keeps Iran from not cheating more on the JCPOA and one of the only things that got them to sign it.

But I want to focus on the gentleman from California's idea of buying a nuclear weapon. He mentions Pakistan, but Pakistan might well listen to their friends in Saudi Arabia. If they have a bomb for sale maybe they would sell it there. They are a Middle Eastern country, or nearly one, and would be directly affected.

I want to focus a little bit about our friends in North Korea. The death of Kim Jong Nam illustrates that we should never have taken North Korea off of the State Sponsors of Terrorism list. North Korea provided the kit that was used to create a nuclear bomb-making facility that was destroyed by Israel, located in Syria, destroyed by Israel last decade. Do any of our panelists have any idea how much money North Korea got in return, not for a nuclear weapon but just a kit to build one, technology? I am seeing four shaking heads.

But I would point out that North Korea is in need of cash. Iran has some already loaded on pallets wrapped in cellophane. And I know that Iran would want the indigenous capacity. I know that they would want more than one weapon. But will any of you comment on why has Iran not purchased a weapon from North Korea? Knowing now that North Korea has a few more weapons than they need to defend themselves from us, they could afford to part with one. Mr. Albright.

Mr. ALBRIGHT. Yes, I think there is worry. I mean, and a nuclear weapon can be transferred in different ways. It doesn't have to be a fully commissioned, workable——

Mr. SHERMAN. Yes, it could be just the fissile, they could sell the fissile material, they could sell the weapon, they could sell——

Mr. ALBRIGHT. That is right. And I think there is a lot of worry.

Mr. SHERMAN [continuing]. The two separately.

Mr. ALBRIGHT. Yes, and I think there is a lot of worry and I think it needs to be looked at, just what is the level of cooperation? I mean I don't know of any credible evidence right now saying that Iran and North Korea are cooperating on nuclear weapons related or nuclear weapons issues, but there is a lot of cooperation on missiles. They have common enemies. And I think it needs to be looked at much more——

Mr. SHERMAN. Do any of you have an opinion on whether the Syria-North Korea transaction of last decade would have inevitably involved Iranian observers, advisers, or cash? Anyone have an opinion on that?

Mr. ALBRIGHT. There has been statements or some evidence that Iran would have had some involvement in it. I was never able to confirm direct involvement. But given the closeness of Iran and Syria, fortunately that reactor doesn't exist anymore and there could certainly, cooperation could——

Mr. SHERMAN. I am going to try to sneak in one more question which is indulgent of the chairman, but on the comment that we need to prevent U.S. banks from financing any aircraft sales to Iran because that creates an incentive for U.S. banks to come here and lobby us in favor of Iran to make sure they get repaid.

The press reports are of discussions of a $10 billion military hardware deal between Russia and Iran including tanks, artillery, and aircraft. The JCPOA says Iran can't buy those kinds of weapons without the approval of a secret, five-member committee that operates in secret but we have a seat on that and can veto such sales. Is there any possibility that the United States would approve or fail to veto, any transfer of weapons from Russia to Iran?

Mr. ALBRIGHT. I don't think so. If I can say the problem is that the ban ends after 5 years or earlier if the IAEA issues its broader conclusion on the additional protocols. So really, this duration issue transcends nuclear to conventional and ballistic missile and it is something the Trump administration is going to have to factor in strongly into its policy review on Iran of how do we deal with these exemptions that in essence take place in not that distant future.

Mr. SHERMAN. Okay. I will give one more comment and then I will yield back. No, I will yield back.

Chairman ROYCE. Let's do this.

Mr. SHERMAN. I will yield back.

Chairman ROYCE. Let's get back to 5 minutes and let's start with Steve Chabot on that from Ohio. Thanks.

Mr. CHABOT. Thank you for your indulgence. As we all know, ultimately the President became aware because most of us didn't like or agree with the Iran deal and ended up taking action on his own. And some would argue that the previous administration, the Obama administration, had so much invested in the deal that they overlooked provocative actions, overlooked, arguably, a whole series of flagrant violations of the deal itself, and Iran pretty much got away with murder, I think, literally in some cases, but figuratively also.

I would just like to go down the line and see, what do you think of what a lot of people think about this, the fact that the administration did overlook far too much, some of those things which you have already commented on here today, because this was one of their great accomplishments, something some people thought couldn't be done.

So I will start with you, Ms. Bauer.

Ms. BAUER. In terms of potential violations on the margins of the JCPOA, I think it is important to consider proportional responses. In my testimony there is a section where I look at the use of proportional responses to what the previous administration may have called "deviations" in terms of compliance with the deal, but what this administration might be more inclined to call "violations."

And so I think it is important to have options available short of abrogating the deal. Those could be things like not approving decisions that come in front of the Joint Commission or suspending licensing, not the licenses themselves perhaps, but suspending licensing under the agreement until such issues are resolved.

Mr. CHABOT. Mr. Albright.

Mr. ALBRIGHT. I think my criticisms are fairly well known. I thought that conditions should have been stronger in many cases. I mean I did not support the deal despite a lobbying effort on the part of the administration. And I had supported publicly the JPA, but I thought there were several cases, conditions that just weren't strong enough where I could support them. I didn't come out against it.

I have since, with implementation, become more critical of that. I think too many concessions were made, many more noes should have been given rather than yeses, and I think it has made this situation more difficult to deal with. And one of the challenges of the Trump administration is going to be to reverse this, and I think it is going to be challenging.

And I think the things I put in my testimony, the short term things, are the things to do today. I mean obviously you can't get them all, but there are a lot of opportunities to start changing the nature of the implementation that can start today and the U.S. has the power to do it. But I do think it is going to be tough.

And then there is this issue of, there are these problems, I mentioned one, and Congressman Rohrabacher in a sense is alluding to them, that the duration is a real problem in this agreement. I mean I wish 10 years was a long period of time in the Middle East, but it is not. And in some sense the major limitations of the deal start to unwind quicker than it took to negotiate this deal, if you go back to the start point as 2003.

And so you have a real problem of how does now the administration deal with these conditions that are going to unwind in the future with conventional weapons, ballistic missiles——

Mr. CHABOT. Thank you. Let me cut you off there because some of us are being held to 5 minutes.

Mr. ALBRIGHT. Okay, I apologize.

Mr. CHABOT. Mr. Modell.

Mr. MODELL. No, to a couple of things to Mr. Rohrabacher's point, I think that the deal is actually a large setback to those in and outside of Iran who were eager to see us to actually do things that would lead to momentum for channeling resistance against the regime.

And I think, you know, everything from 2009 when the Green Movement started happening and there was a moratorium on dealing with members of the Green Movement and actually aiding people as they were trying to channel resentment and figure out how to take disparate clusters of resistance and form an actual resistance movement for the first time in 35 years at the time, it was a tremendous failing and it was all in the interest of ill-conceived rapprochement in the nuclear deal.

I won't comment on the nuclear deal in particular, but the one thing I think it is important to consider is that the deal itself—in a sense from an intel perspective or a law enforcement perspective—was a real setback, because now everyone is so eager to preserve the deal that we are putting the brakes on and we are cautiously walking around the idea of law enforcement. The verification of this still is critical. And I think to the extent that the CIA and the intelligence community were actually on the right path of developing better ways of working with law enforcement—detecting, disrupting, and dismantling counter proliferation networks—there has been a setback to that degree. And I think now we have an uphill climb in terms of verification and counter proliferation.

Mr. CHABOT. Thank you. Mr. Chairman, my time has expired. Can Dr. Exum respond? I leave it up to you.

Mr. EXUM. Mr. Chairman, with permission, could I briefly respond?

Chairman ROYCE. Yes.

Mr. EXUM. Thank you so much, Mr. Chairman. First off, Congressman, I believe we overestimated the degree to which the diplomatic channel we established between Secretary Kerry and Zarif who could bear fruit outside of the nuclear negotiations. I think we thought it could, bottom line is it didn't. They didn't want to talk about anything except for the nuclear deal.

Second, in terms of pushing back against other things Iran was doing, there were lots of reasons having nothing to do with the nuclear deal why we didn't. In Syria, the President as you all know took several options off the table in terms of what we could do in Syria. In Iraq we had a fight against the Islamic State to prosecute that we didn't want to endanger by pushing back against Iran too soon. And then third, in Yemen, I don't think the administration wanted to get drawn any deeper into Yemen. It is actually in Yemen and specifically with respect to the threat to freedom of navigation where I think we could have been more aggressive and think that would have made sense.

Chairman ROYCE. We now go to Mr. Greg Meeks of New York. Mr. MEEKS. Thank you, Mr. Chairman. And let me just say, first of all, I appreciate the opportunity to be able to examine our policy toward Iran. I think that this will be our seventh full committee hearing on Iran in the past year, and I appreciate the opportunity to understand the threat that Iran poses to the Middle East and I know that we will have further questions.

However, I must also say with the ongoing new administration and President Trump's bizarre policies toward Mr. Putin and Russia, as you have said, Mr. Chairman that Russia has demonstrated that the hope of cooperation cannot survive the cold calculation of his narrow interests, I would hope that and I know that we are going to have some hearing on Russia in a couple of weeks or so, but I hope that we have more focus on Russia and its involvement because it seems to be threatening our very democracy.

It has come out clearly about the Russian involvement in our elections for the President of the United States here in America, and Russia's involvement in France and in Germany and those elections there. It seems to me that there is a great threat of what Russia is doing around the world.

And being a committee that has gotten together and, you know, I see the Senate is starting to move on that side in a bipartisan way to start talking about where Russia is and what Russia is doing, whether it is in Iran or other places around the world, and what the connections are between Russia and our current administration, because it seems as though every day there are more ties to Russia's intelligence services that are being discovered at the highest level of our national security apparatus.

So I would think that this committee, and one of the things that I do like about this committee is that we work in a bipartisan way. That we would be the committee, since it does not seem that anybody on the House side, and I do see some senators on the other side of the aisle starting to talk about doing something, but I would hope that—and I don't hear any committee or anything being done on the House side. I know that when we had Benghazi, et cetera, there was other committees that stood up and did certain things at their end for investigation.

I would hope then that the Foreign Affairs Committee in a bipartisan way would step up and say, "there is a threat to our democracy," and we hold many hearings. In fact we could lead Congress in coming together to say that we are going to look into what is happening in Russia and Russia's narrow interest in how they are affecting us here in the United States of America.

And look at what the President's positions have been and the people that are affiliated with him, because just recently, just even yesterday it comes out that even during the campaign there has been many individuals from the Trump campaign that had some contact with Russia. And clearly when we had General Flynn, who had to leave because of his connections with Russia.

So I think that it provides a unique opportunity for us to have some continuous hearings on Russia, its relationship and contact with the United States, what it is doing, what it is not doing, its connections with the current administration. That conversation is very important to every American whether you are Democrat, whether you are Republican, whether you are Independent, it is something that I think is going to the heart.

And as the camera of history rolls it will be looking back on what did we do in the United States Congress? What did we do at the time that our own democracy was threatened by outside entity? Did we fully investigate and go into it as an independent body, a separate branch of government to make sure that we have done everything to protect ourselves?

So, you know, it is good that we and we could even talk about—
—

Chairman ROYCE. Will the gentleman yield?

Mr. MEEKS. We could even talk about, and I am not going to get a minute left, but I know we only get five.

Chairman ROYCE. I understand.

Mr. MEEKS. We could even talk about, you know, Russia, you know, and I think we have had some of these conversations about Russia and its involvement with reference to Iran, of clearly, you know, we have heard questions here today talking about Russia providing ballistic missiles to Iran. We have talked and heard about that had Russia, had discussions over $10 billion in military hardware. So that is, you know, a problem to us even as you talk about dealing with Iran.

And then when you figure out, you know, Russia and the consequences of the U.S. and Russian cooperation which has, you know, this administration has expressed openness to U.S. cooperation with Russia in Syria and how does that affect us in Iran and can you do an agreement with Russia? What is this deal with Russia and this administration?

We have got to get to the bottom of this, and I think there is nothing more important for us as members of the legislative branch and the Foreign Affairs Committee for us to focus on where, what, when, and how Russia is involved with this administration. I yield back.

Chairman ROYCE. Well, thank you, and I thank the gentleman for yielding. Even before this week's events I have been discussing with Ranking Member Engel a hearing focused on the way in which Russia works to undermine Western democracies including the United States, including France and Germany, and including efforts to undermine NATO. As the intelligence reports from January noted, they did that here. They will do it again in the upcoming European elections in France and Germany.

So it is appropriate that we hear from experts on the appropriate steps to be taken in response and this will continue the critical oversight role that our committee has played on U.S.-Russia policy. I will remind the members that we have had hearings specifically on Russia and its aggressive acts in the past and, after all, this is the committee that led the way to impose sanctions on Russia. We did that after its invasion of Ukraine. And this is the committee that has been sounding the alarm about Russia's weaponization of information if you go through the hearings that we have had on RT, and I would expect that to be the first hearing we hold after next week's recess, as I have shared with Mr. Engel.

So I appreciate the gentleman's observations and we now go to Ileana Ros-Lehtinen of Florida.

Ms. ROS-LEHTINEN. Thank you so much, Chairman Royce and Ranking Member Engel, for continuing to focus on the real and serious threat of Iran. As recent events have indicated and as you both have pointed out, Iran's provocative actions have not subsided in this post nuclear deal world and in fact, in many aspects, its illicit activity seems to have been on the rise. Iran remains a direct threat to our national security, to our friend and ally the democratic Jewish

State of Israel, and to the stability of the entire Middle East.

Often lost in the discussion of the JCPOA or Iran's ballistic missile test is how closely this all mirrors North Korea's nuclear and ballistic missile programs. Our Middle East Subcommittee has convened several hearings on this topic in the last few weeks. North Korea and Iran have been suspected of having some level of nuclear cooperation; at the very least, Iran learned from the North Korea playbook on how to win concessions from the West and still get its nuclear weapons.

For certain these two rogue regimes have a long history of collaboration on ballistic missile development. Iran's latest test was apparently a ballistic missile of North Korean origin. This is a very dangerous alliance, we must not continue to view Iran and North Korea as two separate tracks. We have the Iran, North Korea, and

Syria Nonproliferation Act, INKSNA, which now could be a valuable tool to prevent proliferation of nuclear, radiological, chemical, or ballistic missile material to these regimes. Unfortunately, the previous administration was severely deficient in its reporting requirements under INKSNA. A GAO report found that the administration was years behind in its reporting, years behind, which had the unfortunate consequence of delaying sanctions on proliferation activities by Iran. By doing so, the previous administration effectively blocked key sanctions against Iran while the nuclear negotiations were ongoing, much to our detriment.

In order to be effective we must fully and vigorously enforce sanctions and we must look at ways of expanding them if we are to curb Iran's dangerous actions. This includes, Mr. Chairman and Mr. Ranking Member, rigorous enforcement of the JCPOA and it includes reimposing some sanctions lifted by the JCPOA that fell under more than just nonproliferation sanctions. That is why I will introduce my Iran, North Korea, and Syria Nonproliferation Accountability Act which will modify the existing law and give us greater flexibility to hold these regimes and those individuals and entities accountable for the proliferation of their illicit activity. So I ask the panel kindly, could you tell us a little bit more about the Iran-North Korea nexus and what that proliferation network looks like, especially as it relates to their ballistic missile collaboration?

And finally, Mr. Albright, you discussed Iran repeatedly taking advantage of loopholes and going over the threshold on heavy water and low enriched uranium. For what purpose would Iran need to enrich more than the alloted 300 kilogram cap on low enriched uranium or 130 metric tons of heavy water?

Thank you, Mr. Chairman and Mr. Ranking Member.

Mr. ALBRIGHT. It is very hard to penetrate the Iran-North Korean cooperation. I think it is better left to closed hearings to really get into that. I mean one thing that can be said though, and it is a little bit of an answer to an earlier question, is I think it is very important for the United States to sanction companies in Europe and in China that are linked to providing goods to Iran and North Korea.

And I bring up the European side of this mainly because it is very hard for the European countries now to do that. Their sanctions or listing of companies can be challenged quite easily because of the nature of their system, and I think it is important that the U.S. sanction European and Chinese companies.

Now in terms of taking advantage of the loopholes, and I listed several, now why would it need to enrich more? I mean I don't think it does. I think it just wants to push the envelope, create precedence. It wants to undermine the limitations of the JCPOA that were, at least from the U.S. point of view, intended to be pretty robust on that limit. They want to be able to justify why they would need a large gas centrifuge program, and one of the ways they are going to try to do it is by developing an indigenous fuel fabrication capability that uses low enriched uranium which of course has to be tested, you have to go above the limit to make more enriched uranium for the test fuel.

And by doing that when the international community would want to stop enrichment, the justification for the enrichment would be deeply embedded in a civil nuclear argumentation whether that is the original or the ultimate intention or not.

So I think again it is for Iran——

Ms. Ros-Lehtinen. Thank you, sir, I am sorry, I was long-winded and ran out of time.

Thank you, Mr. Chairman.

Chairman Royce. Thank you.

Ms. Ros-Lehtinen. Thank you, sir. Thank you, again.

Chairman Royce. Mr. Gerry Connolly of Virginia.

Mr. Connolly. Thank you, Mr. Chairman. And I appreciate the chairman's recitation of groundbreaking work done by this committee on Russia and I agree with him. I guess the concern on this side of the aisle that could easily be reassured is moving forward. Minority wrote——

Chairman Royce. If the gentleman would yield.

Mr. Connolly. Only if he suspends my time. If you suspend my time I am happy to yield, because you only give me 5 minutes.

Chairman Royce. Mr. Connolly, go ahead with whatever points you want to make.

Mr. Connolly. All right. Three months ago, the minority wrote a letter to Eliot Engel, the ranking member, asking him to deliver it to the chairman asking for an immediate hearing even before the inauguration on this Russia connection. We have, to my knowledge, not received the reply.

Earlier this week, Mr. Cicilline and all of the Democrats signed a letter asking that General Flynn be brought before this committee so this committee can examine the foreign policy implications of what just happened. And I certainly look forward to an answer on that request. So I associate myself with remarks of Mr. Meeks that moving forward that is what we are concerned about. And I continue to hear gratuitous slaps at the previous administration on the subject of Iran because the agreement wasn't all encompassing. Dr. Exum, are bilateral agreements between us and another country, are they typically all encompassing? Is that the record?

Mr. Exum. No, they are not. And in this case we again, this one particularly——

Mr. Connolly. So when we sign nuclear, well, going back to the very first nuclear test ban treaty during the Kennedy administration with the then Soviet Union, you mean those agreements did not address human rights violations or Jewish immigration or Gulags or misbehavior in other parts of the world that were causing us great grief?

Mr. Exum. Not only that, Congressman, I seem to recall that we still faced significant conventional overmatch in the continent of Europe.

Mr. Connolly. So, well, certainly the JCPOA has failed though, Dr. Exum, isn't that right? I mean every single metric set by the JCPOA has been violated by Iran or they have cheated, and we have caught them at it, right?

Mr. Exum. Well, I think with respect to the JCPOA I think that there is room to push back against Iran in a more robust way, but we ought to do so with caution.

Mr. CONNOLLY. Dr. Exum, is there a single metric they have not reached?

Mr. EXUM. I am not, I would defer to the Energy Department and to the Department of——

Mr. CONNOLLY. Enrichment of uranium—they reached the goal. The Iraq production facility, plutonium reactor—they filled it with cement. Shipping enriched material out of the country—they did it. You know, inspections—they have done it. I mean by all accounts they have pretty much met the metrics. Now we have to monitor it, and I agree with my friends on the other side of the aisle. In fact, I have introduced legislation that would create a Helsinki-like commission to do just that so it is hopefully removed from politics and partisanship.

But compliance obviously remains an issue, but you can't argue that the JCPOA has been a failure. And that is why after hearing all of the predictions for a year or more of how it would fail and they would cheat and by the way it would accelerate them as a nuclear power, surely you would agree that is not what happened. They are not closer to nuclear development today than before the JCPOA, are they?

Mr. EXUM. No, that is exactly right. Now Mr. Albright may have more to add, but as far as I——

Mr. CONNOLLY. I only have 1 minute and 24, and I have a feeling the chairman is going to be strict about it, so let me talk about the Russian connection. How about we talk about the new President.

Mr. EXUM. Sure.

Mr. CONNOLLY. And I listened with interest to your testimony. In some ways this Russia connection makes it harder, not easier, for us to try to deter or address Iranian behavior, does it not?

Mr. EXUM. Well, I believe it absolutely does.

Mr. CONNOLLY. Please explicate.

Mr. EXUM. Well, especially with respect to Syria, I think we have seen many disturbing, and on the one hand the coalition in Syria they are not as, the opposing coalition in Syria they are not as stable as our own counter-Daesh coalition is, so there are some fissures between the Russians and the Iranians, for example, or between Hezbollah and the Russians.

But I am growing increasingly alarmed by the degree to which their coalition activities in Syria have brought Russia and Iran closer together. We have certainly seen just images on social media of Russian Spetznosts on the ground in Syria with Hezbollah patches on in a way that alarms us in the same way that U.S. special operators on the ground in northeast Syria working with Kurdish groups alarms the Turks.

And I think quite frankly we have reason to believe that Russia's introduction and escalation in Syria in the fall of 2015 made it more difficult, not easier, to push back against what Iran was doing in Syria and elsewhere in the region, sir.

Mr. CONNOLLY. I thank you.

Chairman ROYCE. We go now to Mr. Joe Wilson of South Carolina.

Mr. WILSON. Thank you, Mr. Chairman, and I appreciate you and Ranking Member Eliot Engel for your bipartisan approach to the issues that we are facing concerning Iran. I am grateful that we had a bipartisan success in adding language to the National Defense Authorization Act to require an analysis of Iranian missile testing.

The Trump administration took a good first step in designating Iranian missile proliferation networks in response to the recent tests. More needs to be done. And for Ms. Bauer, what are your recommendations for near and short term actions to address Iran's ballistic missile system?

Ms. BAUER. Thank you. I think there are a lot of options to use the existing authority. It is like the authority that was invoked in last month's action to continue to identify procurement networks. What is especially impactful can be targeting those previously non-public affiliations between commercial fronts and Iranian actors, because these front companies need to operate, they need to appear to be legitimate in order to procure dual use goods. They need to hold bank accounts, and exposing this publicly can be incredibly disruptive.

Mr. WILSON [presiding]. And I appreciate that. And of course what they are doing violates U.N. resolutions too, so it really is insulting in light of the Iranian nuclear deal that everything seems to continue. In fact, Mr. Albright, apologists for the dangerous nuclear deal claim, "If Iran cheats, we will know it." I agree with Mr. Rohrabacher earlier who said this is wishful thinking which puts American families at risk of attack. What is your assessment?

Mr. ALBRIGHT. In the short term, with the program rolled back quite a bit the chance of detecting cheating is pretty good, but in the longer term I would say it is not. And that is why it is critical to, in a sense, really deal with this issue of access by the IAEA. Iran will have greater incentives to cheat in the future if it now can limit the ability of the IAEA to access.

And in the longer term, I mean I don't think this deal can be verified after a certain number of rollbacks in the conditions. If you are talking 10, 15 years from now, I think it will be extremely difficult to verify this arrangement if Iran builds up its nuclear program as it stated it is going to build up.

Mr. WILSON. Well, to me it is such wishful thinking, the notification, the number of days we have to provide, the fact that there are no Americans serving on the inspection teams. This is beyond wishful thinking. It is putting the American families at risk.

Mr. Modell, Obama administration officials repeatedly incorrectly testified that the dangerous nuclear agreement would in no way impact our pressing Iran on human rights and sanctioning those responsible for the brutal treatment of the Iranian people. However, there have been no designations for human rights abuses since the nuclear deal was implemented despite continued calls from Congress to do so. What specific steps can the new administration take to press Iran on human rights?

Mr. MODELL. First of all, in terms of the first thing is listing individuals for human rights abuses. The second thing though, and I have spent a great amount of time here on human rights abuses and terrorism and the other violations of the Iranian regime, but on human rights in particular is to use the media tools that we are funding that we are spending millions of dollars on every year to highlight those things and to make it an integral part of U.S. policy pressuring the regime from the outside.

Mr. WILSON. And I appreciate so much Mr. Rohrabacher pointing out that the prior administration, we had such an opportunity with the Green Revolution. I had many friends in South Carolina, of all things, Iranian-Americans who had such hopes for regime change to give opportunity to the extraordinary people of the culture of Persia, to be under a theocracy that is so debilitating and so threatening to all the neighbors. And with two sons who served in Iraq, I know firsthand where the IEDs came from, and anyone who has faced that understands.

And this really follows too, something never to be forgotten and that was the bombing of the Beirut Marine barracks. Hundreds, 283, I believe, Americans murdered and it was by the Iranian regime, the largest explosive device since Hiroshima and Nagasaki. It should not be forgotten.

I now yield to Mr. Deutch of Florida.

Mr. DEUTCH. I thank the chairman. First, Mr. Modell, I want to thank you for bringing up the issue of Iran's abduction of Iranian-Americans and dual nationals.

I would also like to take this opportunity to note that March 9th will mark the 10th anniversary that my constituent Bob Levinson went missing off of Kish Island. And as I have said at every hearing that we have had about Iran, that has to continue to be Issue 1 in every discussion that we have with the Iranians. There is a new administration here, and I urge this administration just as I urged the last administration to make this a very important priority. And I appreciate you raising the issue.

Mr. Albright, you criticized the IAEA for a lack of transparency. I am very concerned about that as well. My understanding is that the new administration hasn't reached out to the IAEA yet to discuss its monitoring of Iran. Clearly that is a problem. They need to hear from our representatives to the IAEA. There needs to be an exhaustive discussion with the coordinator for Iran nuclear implementation, whom I understand still holds that position. The administration should do that, but I also, Mr. Chairman, would urge this committee in order to tackle the issue of transparency to request that our representatives to the IAEA and the coordinator come to testify here in front of us to address specifically the transparency issues that Mr. Albright has raised. They are very serious. They will impact not just this deal in this year, but as Mr. Albright rightly points out, as the deal carries on for the remainder of its term. So Mr. Chairman, I hope that you will consider that.

And finally, Dr. Exum, I want to just spend my remaining couple of minutes talking to you about the "strategic flirtation," I think is how you referred to it, that this administration has engaged in with Russia. Before getting specifically to Russia and Iran that flirtation also takes place as there is a Russian spy ship off of our coast and as there is a mock attack on a U.S. destroyer in the Black Sea and at a time when Russia has now deployed a cruise missile, and then focus with that as background focus on Iran for a minute.

How do we engage in the ways that this administration has seemed intent on doing with Russia while Iran has thousands of fighters and proxies like Hezbollah fighting alongside the Russians in Iran and as this committee and this Congress look at additional sanctions outside of the nuclear area, Iran's support for terrorism, for example, how do we do that in an effective way when we are simultaneously engaged in this new relationship with Russia that weakens our ability to do what we need to?

Mr. EXUM. Well, thank you, Congressman. I will be blunt. I don't think you can do it. I think that—and I am unfortunately the veteran of many weeks spent across a negotiating table with Russians in Geneva over the last year trying to find some way forward on the conflict in Syria. We conducted these negotiations as Russia was enabling the destruction of East Aleppo and the slaughter of thousands of Syrian civilians. We did so in an effort to determine whether or not Russia might be some sort of partner in Syria, whether they could use their leverage over the regime, over Iran, over Hezbollah, to broker some sort of peace in Syria.

And at the conclusion of that quite bluntly, Congressman, I don't think that Russia necessarily has the influence over the Syrian regime to be able to broker any type of peace. And I think that frankly Russia and the Iranians have more common cause than they do any strategic disagreements.

So for me again, Congressman, I just don't see the administration's outreach toward Russia, I just don't see how they can do that without strengthening the Iranian hand in Syria, without strengthening the Iranian hand regionally, without strengthening the hand of groups like Hezbollah which pose a clear threat to the state of Israel, and without emboldening groups like Hezbollah and these Iranian-backed PMF that potentially pose a threat to U.S. forces in Iraq in addition to the Iraqi state.

Mr. DEUTCH. I appreciate that.

Mr. Chairman, just before I yield back I would note for the record the reason that it is so important to engage immediately in a bipartisan investigation into the relationship between the White House and Russia is not just because of leaks, which seems to be the President's biggest concern, but because of the policy implications that stretch not just to U.S., Russia, and our discussions with our NATO allies, but all the way to Iran and the threats against the United States and our allies in the region that Russia may be contributing to. And with that I yield back.

Mr. WILSON. And thank you, Mr. Deutch. We now yield to the judge, Congressman Ted Poe of Texas.

Mr. POE. I thank the chairman. I am going to talk about Iran which is I think the basis of this hearing. Maybe we will have a hearing on Russia at some point.

I think we gave away the farm, the mineral rights, when we made the Iranian deal. I couldn't disagree with you more, Dr. Exum, about the Iranian deal. It was a bad deal for the United States. We gave them $150 billion that they should not have gotten. I believe that money did not go to build schools and hospitals in Iran, it went to the IRGC which runs 80 percent of the economy, and the IRGC funds terrorist operations throughout the world, namely with their proxy group Hezbollah.

So I want to talk about Iran not Russia, and Iran and their status in the world today. One of you mentioned rules of engagement, hopefully we will change the rules of engagement with Iran. I hope that we do and we don't find ourselves in another situation like in the last administration on January the 10th or 12th of 2016 when two of our river command boats surrendered to the Iranians, surrendered.

So much for the American phrase, "Don't give up the ship. We gave up two ships to the Iranians, and Secretary Kerry almost apologized. We still haven't gotten the facts of that situation. Maybe we will change the rules of engagement where we don't allow Iranians to capture our ships without a fight over in that part of the world.

But I want to talk about the IRGC. Do you think that the IRGC has planned and executed terrorist attacks throughout the world including against Americans, Mr. Modell?

Mr. MODELL. Thank you for the questions, Congressman. I don't that there is any doubt whatsoever that the IRGC, particularly the Quds Force, has planned terrorist activities against the U.S. and U.S forces, U.S. persons, and its allies around the world. I think between 2012 and 2015, there were at least 30 such activities that were in some way traced back to the IRGC. So I don't think that there is any doubt about that whatsoever.

Mr. POE. Does the IRGC have training camps in Iran that train other people from other parts of the world in terrorist activities? Mr.

MODELL. I think the publicly available information would point you to Iranian sponsored and run training camps in southern Lebanon.

Are there training camps in Iran? I think that is probably meant for discussion in a more private setting.

Mr. POE. Well, how about in South America? How about South America, can you answer that question?

Mr. MODELL. South America, beyond the rumors of Iranian training camps in Margarita Island and certain parts of Venezuela I have not heard of anything. I have heard of Iranian outreach in various nefarious ways to certain groups in Latin America, but the links between for instance the Vice President of Venezuela and Iran have been long discussed and long, there has been a lot of speculation about links therein to terrorism and destabilizing activity——

Mr. POE. How about the Iranian sponsor of Hezbollah in Syria and Lebanon?

Mr. MODELL. I don't think there is any doubt about that.

Mr. POE. That it happens. I mean they sponsor the terrorist group Hezbollah.

Mr. MODELL. Not only do they sponsor the terrorist group Hezbollah, but I can tell you when Syria began in full force and Iran really started to take a leading role, Hezbollah actually put up some resistance and said we are not sure that we really want to become embroiled in this, and the Iranians strong-armed them and said yeah, you are going to do that. So it is not a matter of Iran supporting or sponsoring them, it is about them controlling them to a large extent.

Mr. POE. Do you think that the IRGC based on their activities worldwide and their sponsorship of terrorism should be back on the list or on the list as a sponsor of terrorism, that the Treasury Department should designate them as a terrorist organization? Just want your opinion.

Mr. MODELL. In my opinion, I don't think so. I don't think so. I think that there are certain parts of the IRGC that should be and the Quds Force. I don't think that the original purpose of the designations for foreign terrorist organizations were meant for entire militaries, and that is essentially what the IRGC is. I think it is overreach and I think, actually I don't think it will have much of an impact.

Mr. POE. I am not asking for a foreign terrorist organization designation, I am asking if you think that the Treasury Department under their power should designate it as a terrorist organization. It is a different designation.

Mr. MODELL. Treasury designating the IRGC as a terrorist organization makes sense just given the depth of IRGC involvement in all facets of Iranian terrorism, so yes, in that regard it is. It would be sensible, yes.

Mr. POE. I am out of time, I yield back. Thank you very much.

Chairman ROYCE. Mr. Cicilline of Rhode Island.

Mr. CICILLINE. Thank you, Mr. Chairman. I want to thank you for calling this hearing. Now more than ever the United States must show the world that we are serious about holding Iran to account and enforcing the JCPOA as well as examining Iran's destabilizing activities around the world. But it is impossible to talk about Iran and not talk about Russia, particularly when you consider Russia's blocking of sanctions against Iran at the U.N., and Russia's support of Iranian activities in Syria.

But I fear that we are at a disadvantage when we have a President who seems unable and unwilling to stand up to Vladimir Putin, Iran's biggest supporter and patron. As the body in the House responsible for our foreign policy it is incumbent upon us to examine the very real consequences of President Trump's pivot toward Russia and what that means for our national security, our relationships with allies, and the function of our own Government.

Mr. Chairman, it has been 8 months since we had a full committee hearing on Russia. I believe we are long overdue, and we must have witnesses from the administration appear before us and give a full and honest accounting of what their plans are for dealing with this unprecedented Russian aggression and meddling in the United States.

Moreover, as the body tasked with oversight of our foreign diplomacy apparatus, we absolutely must require General Michael Flynn to appear before this committee and answer truthfully about what his relationship and contacts were with Russian officials before and during his tenure as national security adviser. The issue impacts the United States' relationship with our friends and foes around the world. If we cannot be an honest broker in our dealings with Russia we lose credibility everywhere.

And that is why 19 of my colleagues on this committee and I sent you a letter asking that we have Michael Flynn testify before this committee as soon as possible. I ask unanimous consent that a copy of this letter be entered into the record.

Chairman ROYCE. Without objection.

Mr. CICILLINE. This request is made in the context of the following facts: Unprecedented Russian interference in our elections directed by Vladimir Putin to help elect Donald Trump as concluded by 17 intelligence agencies; a sophisticated plan of hacking, fake news, and a sophisticated use of propaganda; repeated contacts between the Trump campaign and Russians during the course of the campaign. Three members of President Trump's inner circle—Carter Page, Paul Manafort, and now Michael Flynn—have had to leave the inner circle because of their ties to Russian officials. Secret conversations between the national security adviser and the Russian Ambassador, then Michael Flynn lied to the American people, lied to the Vice President of the United States, and denied those conversations, those conversations happening right on the day that sanctions were imposed for interfering with the American Presidential elections.

At the same time, Sally Yates, the acting attorney general, brought that information to the attention of the White House counsel and she concluded that he was a compromised individual who could be blackmailed by the Russians. What did they do? Shortly thereafter Sally Yates is fired, Michael Flynn stays in place for 17 days with full access to classified information continuing all of his responsibilities as a national security adviser.

This is in the context of a President who is bellicose and fighting with all of our allies—Mexico, Australia as two most recent examples—but has showered praise on the brutal dictator Vladimir Putin. He maligns our intelligence professionals, compares them to Nazi Germany, and at the same time we learn that Michael Flynn has appeared at a celebration of RT, the single most powerful Russian propaganda machine, and the President has refused to answer questions about his investments or financial dealings in Russia or to produce his tax returns.

Then we learn his son at a real estate conference in 2008 said, and I quote, "Russians make up a pretty disproportionate cross section of a lot of our assets." And then he went on to say, "We see a lot of money pouring in from Russia."

Mr. Chairman, I don't know what else we need to see to fulfill our responsibilities to get to the bottom of this, because we can't have a real conversation about foreign policy or the implications of our relationships with Russia, with Iran, with the rest of the world until we get to the bottom of this.

And so while I am anxious to have a conversation about Iran and anxious to have a conversation about the JCPOA, I am imploring this committee, Republicans and Democrats, to put your country before party to bring these issues before this committee so we can get to the bottom of this. The American people expect nothing less, and I urge all the members of this committee to join those who have already asked for these hearings, because the American people are watching this and they cannot believe that there hasn't been a bipartisan effort in the House of Representatives to get to what has been unprecedented interference in our democratic institutions, that the sanctity of our democracy, our ability to defend our very way of life is at stake.

And so I don't have a question for this panel. I thank you for your testimony, but I think this gets to the heart of our ability to continue to be a beacon to the world, a place of democracy, of self government, where foreign governments have no role in helping to pick our leaders or interfering with policies that we implement in America. And I thank you and I yield back my remaining 2 seconds.

Chairman ROYCE. Mr. Scott Perry of Pennsylvania.

Mr. PERRY. Thank you, Mr. Chairman. I want to talk about the issue at hand, but I, as you know, simply can't just let the statements of the past remain on their own without correcting the record.

And as long as credibility has been brought up especially by the other side of the aisle, for my whole life, for literally my entire life, I have watched many of my friends on the other side of the aisle or that side of the aisle sidle up to and speak glowingly of horrible dictators like Fidel Castro and——

Chairman ROYCE. Will the gentleman yield for a minute? Just in the interest of comity maybe let me make this point. Mr. Engel and I have already indicated that the first hearing we are going to do is on this issue after the recess when we come back. So for the members here what I would just urge is that we have a panel of experts before us and if we can stay focused on the issue at hand I think that will allow us, especially with the time and effort and expertise that these four individuals have put into studying this problem, allow us to come to some solutions which this committee can then push.

In the meantime, we can prepare for the upcoming hearing in 2 weeks and we are to deal with the issue, an issue which we have long dealt with on this committee, but I would just urge that from members on both sides of the aisle so that we can get back on topic on something that is quite a challenge. And then in 2 weeks we will continue with the good work of this committee and hopefully in a bipartisan way. And with that I will yield back to General Perry.

Mr. PERRY. Thank you, Mr. Chairman. I appreciate your indulgence and I will bring this back home as quickly as I can. I would just point to at least most recently discounting all of my life in watching what I saw. Most recently, regarding Iran and Russia, the Obama administration failed to follow the law and sanction Russia for the sale of the S300 missile system and various other weapons system, aircraft, armored vehicles, et cetera—nary a word. Not a word. Russia invades Crimea—nothing. Nothing from that side. The full outrage and concern is what it is, and I would say this as an old soldier.

Mr. DEUTCH. Will the gentleman yield?

Mr. PERRY. I will not yield. I just want to say this is complementary fashion, in complementary fashion, and it doesn't apply to everybody. It doesn't apply to everybody. But in complementary fashion, welcome to the war. With that Dr. Exum, thank you for your service to the country.

I would also like to refer to the remarks of the gentleman from California, Mr. Rohrabacher, while we discuss the margin, the marginal errors of the agreement or of Iran's actions, the small infractions, whether it is low enriched uranium, heavy water stockpiling, ballistic missile activities, the purchase of conventional weapons, et cetera, I don't think there is any doubt in the room or around the world that in some fashion 10 or 15 years from now Iran is going to be a nuclear armed with delivery capability nation. That is who they are going to be. That is what they are going to be and we are going to deal with that somehow.

And I would also say in agreement with Mr. Rohrabacher, we are not going to go to war with Iran. That is not going to happen. I think the deal is horrible, I always have. It is what it is and we have got to find a way to move forward.

I just want to follow up with you, Mr. Modell, with where Mr. Poe is headed because I was headed there already. What are the ramifications of listing the IRGC as a foreign terrorist organization with specific ties to how Treasury treats their transactions and the permutations of the IRGC and those transactions with other countries, other entities? What are the ramifications if that were to happen? You said you didn't think there would be any, it would be marginal. Can you elaborate on that?

Mr. MODELL. Let me elaborate on that. The part that I think would be not marginal at all would be as it would serve as a significant deterrent to foreign businesses who were looking to get into Iran. So the extent that we can declare them as a foreign terrorist organization by Treasury or by having the State Department continue to add the individuals to the lists that exist, Magnitsky List type of sanctions where we are pointing out corruption and we are actually saying the IRGC's massive commercial enterprise, buyer beware.

So to a large extent the recovery of Iran's economy, the ability of foreign businesses to go in there and actually conduct transactions would be impacted. So perhaps I misspoke, but I think there would be a significant impact economically when you think about the extent to which the IRGC has control over significant sectors of the Iranian economy and to the extent to which such a declaration would probably cause a lot more heartburn among companies that are looking to get in.

Companies that I speak to right now in a private sector capacity—large oil companies, Europeans, multinationals who are looking—the one thing that they ask is say, hey, you guys are based in Washington, DC. We have done a lot of due diligence, we think there is a way we can make a lot of money in Iran, however, there is still this black cloud of sanctions, we don't know where the U.S. is going to go. It is a significant deterrent even when the lawyers have signed off on it and even when people in leading European companies are ready to go back in.

So those types of things give people real pause. So I would stand corrected and say it would have a significant impact.

Mr. PERRY. Thank you, Mr. Chairman. I yield.

Chairman ROYCE. Thank you. I would remind all members that House Rule 17 and committee decorum requires us to confine our remarks to the issues under discussion and to avoid discussion of personality.

And we now go to Dina Titus of Nevada. Thank you.

Ms. TITUS. Thank you, Mr. Chairman.

Dr. Exum, in your testimony you talk about the four Ps strategy that you followed when you were at the Defense Department under the Obama administration—posture, plans, partners, and preparedness. Well, it seems to me under this administration our posture has become negative and hostile, our plans are nonexistent, our partners have all been alienated, and our preparedness is just a state of uncertainty.

We have also heard President Trump when the Iranians circle our beautiful destroyers with their little boats and they make gestures at our people they shouldn't be allowed to make, they will be shot out of the water. We heard this confirmed by one of the members of this committee earlier who was calling for virtual combat on the Gulf coast. We also heard President Trump tell the leadership of Harley Davidson that nothing is off the table when responding to questions about Iran.

Would you just address how this new approach, all this saber rattling is affecting not only our relationship with Iran, but with the other neighbors and potential partners in that part of the world?

Mr. EXUM. Thank you, Congresswoman, for allowing me to address this question. It is a good one. I think for me what worries me most about this current administration, and as I said in my opening statement, I think there are individuals in this administration, Secretary Mattis for example, who come to this administration with deep knowledge of the threat that is posed by Iran as well as the threat to our own troops and our other various equities within the Middle East, and so I have certain faith in certain individuals in this administration.

The two things that worry me, Congresswoman, are first off sequencing. Strategy is often about prioritization and sequencing. And I see some individuals within this administration really eager to pick a fight with Iran. And I think we need to be very careful about how and when we do that if we elect to do that.

Right now we still have a lot of hard fighting in Iraq, for example. We have cleared, with our Iraqi partners, to be clear, have cleared eastern part of Mosul. To clear western Mosul is going to take several, many more months. The Middle Euphrates River Valley still has a significant presence of the Islamic State, and we need to remain focused on that at hand. And I sense within this administration that there are some voices who are so eager to confront Iran that they may not have thought through how exactly they sequence it or what prioritization they are putting into place.

The second thing, and this is really I think the big concern is just the uncertainty within this administration. I don't think that I will surprise anybody here on either side of the aisle by saying that the upheavals we have seen within this administration over the past few weeks have been unprecedented both in terms of personnel, to include the dismissal of the national security adviser, to also include some of the ways in which we have alienated some of our key partners such as—I mean I thought it would take some great effort to offend Australia, but we managed to accomplish it in the first 2 weeks of this administration.

And they are a key partner. They followed us in Vietnam, they are active with us off the coast of the Arabian Peninsula in terms of maritime patrols. We depend on these partners to not only defeat Daesh but also to push back against the threat, the very real threat that my colleagues on this table as well the members of this committee have highlighted in terms of Iran's asymmetric activities.

You know, when we interdict weapons shipments off of the coast of Yemen, for example, it is often not U.S. forces who do this. It is often our partner forces that do this. We need those partners, and right now there is a great deal of uncertainty, I think, among many of them in terms of the strategic direction of this administration in terms of who can speak for this administration, and it is worrying to me both as a former official, but also quite frankly just as an American citizen testifying before this committee today, ma'am.

Ms. TITUS. Thank you.

Yes, Mr. Albright.

Mr. ALBRIGHT. I would like to add I am not part of the administration in any way, but I don't, and there may be some voices trying to pick a fight with Iran, but I don't think they are trying to pick a fight with Iran. I think they are, even with this idea of putting Iran on notice, I mean they, Flynn made clear that they want to have a policy review. They don't have people in place and they need to do a lot of recruitment, but I think, overall I think they are moving ahead rather deliberately. But Iran does things and they have to respond.

Ms. TITUS. Do you think we can have it both ways? We can be cozy with Russia and tough on Iran at the same time?

Mr. ALBRIGHT. On the Russian issue, Iran is——

Ms. TITUS. Thank you, Mr. Chairman. I yield back.

Mr. ALBRIGHT. Okay.

Chairman ROYCE. Thank you. We go now to Mr. Thomas Garrett of Virginia.

Mr. GARRETT. Thank you, Mr. Chairman.

Chairman ROYCE. Mr. Garrett, let's get that microphone closer and make sure you have the red button on.

Mr. GARRETT. Do I get my 10 seconds back? Just kidding. Anybody studying the region with any sort of objectivity understands that the IRGC is the fulcrum of power in Iran. The 2009 uprising failed, I believe, in large part due to what Mr. Sherman, my colleague from California, referenced as a willingness of individuals to level firearms at their fellow citizens. And it wasn't obviously just the IRGC, but subsidiary elements such as the Quds Force thereof. And so if we are attempting to ensure better outcomes in Iran, I think we should focus our efforts on the IRGC. I am not sure if it was Mr. Rohrabacher or Mr. Perry who initially commented on, and actually I think it was Mr. Poe who originally commented on potentially extending the Treasury Department's OFAC controls to implement actions wherein they would treat the IRGC as a sponsor of terror, but I can't think of a good reason not to do this except that as I understand it the JCPOA instructed a lot of the restrictions, a lot of the sanctions that have been placed on the IRGC, to be lifted, which seems to me to be counter to American policy in any number of arenas.

Number one, the previous administration's failure to act in 2015 after the Russians waited 5 years to complete the sale of S300 missiles to Iran created a circumstance wherein if you understand the capabilities of the S300 platform, any generation 4 aircraft carrier based aircraft really can't take off in the Persian Gulf safely. That is just the reality. And so we have no Gen-5 assets, F-35 comments withheld, in that capable range.

And truly I read where we have "a robust suite of plans that are real, resourced, and our forces are ready to execute them," and I wonder if we do, particularly in a world where if we had executed a strike with simply F-22s and B-2s, we have about what, 10 operational platforms of the latter.

So if we wanted to act we couldn't, we know the fulcrum of power in Iran is the IRGC, and we are hamstrung by a JCPOA that doesn't let us attack the fulcrum of power metaphorically, not literally, the IRGC. And it is hard for me to fathom having worn a uniform and knowing Ranger Exum—I use that because it is more impressive than Doctor—and Mr. Perry, fought alongside and served alongside some of the 500 American service members who we estimate were killed by IEDs manufactured by the IRGC and their subsidiaries, which goes beyond the 283 Americans who died in Beirut. And I could keep going, Lebanon, the Khobar Towers, a plot to assassinate the Saudi Ambassador here on this soil.

So if we want a better outcome in Iran I would submit that we need to function in a way that we could penalize the IRGC which will then destabilize the regime because the guns are what keep the mullahs in power. Having said that I would ask, and I don't have a ton of time left, if anybody can tell me if when we do things like send 400 million unmarked euros at a time when it would correlate to the release of foreign held dual citizens—whether it was ransom or not, the optics are bad, right—if that doesn't encourage the same sort of bad behavior? And I would point to similar activities undertaken not just in the Sudan and North Korea subsequent and precedent to that but also in Iran. Here are your foreign nationals back, we have our 400 million, we now have some more people.

So I guess, you know, we have what, U.S. citizens and legal permanent residents to the tune of ten, eight plus two, I think, held in Iran now, and for us to negotiate in good faith I would argue is a betrayal of these folks, of my oath to defend the Constitution and the citizens of the nation that it rules over and how can we do that?

I mean why not just cut off all activities in any nonmilitary way that we can with the fulcrum of power in Iran and refuse to do business with those who do business with these folks and let them choose between economic activities with the United States or with Iran? I think I know which way they would make those choices.

So I guess this is a really convoluted compound question, but doesn't the JCPOA really hamstring us from attacking metaphorically, not literally, the axis of power, the fulcrum of power in Iran, the IRGC, by virtue of the elements therein, and therefore doesn't it actually serve to perpetuate the existence of the regime?

Mr. Modell. Sorry, you just got picked at random.

Mr. MODELL. No, Congressman Garrett, I couldn't agree more. I think that if you are going to actually do the things that Congressman Rohrabacher was talking about and some of things that I mentioned in my testimony—that is weakening the IRGC—you have to focus on that.

And I think the existence of this regime depends on the existence of the IRGC. They are at the center of everything. For them to control 25 to 50 percent of the economy and not to be held accountable or for businesses not to be held to a higher standard before doing business over there, and I think quite frankly the hurdles are way too low, you are actually contributing to the perpetuation of a regime that is fundamentally against us in every way.

Mr. GARRETT. Right. And Mr. Chairman, I know I am over a bit. Did we not with the JCPOA seek to essentially see hopefully regime change through a more moderate regime before the Iranians hit that nuclear threshold? That is really the goal, right? Give us time and if there is a change in the power, but if we don't hit that fulcrum of power there will be no regime change. Mr. Albright?

Mr. ALBRIGHT. Yes. Well, that was some of the talking points. I am not sure the negotiators necessarily believe that, but in a sense they were asking to kick the can down the road and they did.

And on your question on the IRGC I think the impact on the JCPOA is do we lose the Europeans or not. I mean that is really, and so I think the issue for the administration is they are going to have to get out there and manage the relationship with the Europeans so if they do decide to move forward on listing the IRGC under the executive order as a terrorist organization that they don't lose the Europeans, because certainly it is their business that will be affected.

But I think it can be done, but it certainly, the administration has to get out there and talk to them. The Europeans have made it clear that this upsets them, but I think that it can be managed. Ms.

BAUER. Excuse me, if you would indulge me for just a moment. I think that you are right that sanctions diplomacy is very important.

Chairman ROYCE. I am afraid time is expired, but we are going to let you put that in writing.

Ms. BAUER. Okay.

Chairman ROYCE. Let's see, Brad Schneider of Illinois.

Mr. SCHNEIDER. Thank you, Mr. Chairman. And let me just start by thanking the witnesses for your testimony here today and your service to our country and your work across time on this particularly important issue.

Ms. Bauer, I want to emphasize what you talked about in your testimony. I think the three points you made are worth repeating. One, the necessity of taking back the narrative, the need to emphasize the sanctions that are still in place and to enforce those sanctions rigorously, vigorously to the greatest extent possible.

You said in your testimony that sanctions are most effective when they are adopted by international community, the international coalition. My question, and I leave this question with the whole panel, what are the challenges to maintaining, if not strengthening, international support for sanctions and the opportunities to bring increasing bite to the sanctions in place and potential sanctions against Iran's activities not just around ballistic missiles but human rights and their activity in conventional weapons throughout the region?

Ms. BAUER. Thank you. I think that one of the challenges to increasing the bite of sanctions and to rebuilding this multilateral coalition that we had before is that it does largely come down to the Europeans and the view in Europe that an important part of their dialogue with Iran is the commercial dialogue. But they are divided on this point and they in fact do maintain sanctions on the IRGC in Europe under their human rights authorities and they maintain sanctions on Hezbollah's military wing. So they are divided on this issue.

I think what is important going forward from the U.S. perspective in more vigorously enforcing the sanctions we have is that we continue to do those based on conduct, because that will be, continuing to emphasize the ways in which Iran violates international norms will be something that will be helpful in rebuilding a multilateral coalition.

Mr. SCHNEIDER. Mr. Albright, you said with the last question that there is a question, do we lose the Europeans? What steps would increase that likelihood, what steps should we be taking to make sure that we don't lose the Europeans in enforcing sanctions?

Mr. ALBRIGHT. Yes, I think it, and this would reflect just visits in Europe. I mean this when they will say, and maybe it is just the optics of it, the additional signal, but they will say that this would end business between European companies and Iran. I understand what Ms. Bauer said and I would actually defer to her, but what I clearly heard was that there is something going on here that this other designation would cause companies to pull back.

And maybe it is not true. Maybe that will be part of the management is that they should be more careful in the first place based on having these sanctions in the IRGC. But I do think that the administration has to get out there and start discussing these things with them and not just hope for the best.

Mr. SCHNEIDER. I will continue down the panel. Mr. Modell, you are nodding.

Mr. MODELL. No, I would just second that. I would say that we talk to companies all the time that, you know, have signed MOUs and they are on the verge of actually making the leap into Iran and there still is a real fundamental lack of clarity on their part as to what they can and cannot do. Treasury does a great job of laying out some of the dos and don'ts, and there is U.S. Government Web sites where you can go and see what you can and can't do in the sanctions.

But really quite frankly it is cumbersome and it is a lot to get through. There is no nice easy dos and don'ts list for companies. I think there has to be a media offensive that reminds companies of the dangers of doing it. And quite frankly, a lot of companies have gone in there and tripped and fallen and have reputational risk.

There should be some sort of a list, consumer report, some U.S. Government sponsored Web site that actually details bad experiences that companies have had in going in there so that other companies can reach out and say wait a minute, maybe we ought to think about that sounding board, consumer reports if you will. But a lot of companies have experiences that we should exhibiting.

Mr. SCHNEIDER. Dr. Exum, I don't want to leave you out.

Mr. EXUM. Well, sanctions is not my specialty and I plead igno-
rance. I defer to the expertise of the other panelists.

Mr. SCHNEIDER. Well, thank you. I have just a little bit of time left,
but I think, and I had raised these concerns when the JCPOA was
announced the need to make sure that Iran cannot get any closer to
a nuclear weapon during the time frame of the JCPOA or any time
thereafter and indeed make it clear that U.S. policy is Iran will
never have a nuclear weapon. And with that I yield back. Chairman
ROYCE. I thank the gentleman, and we go to Mr. Ted Lieu of California.

Mr. LIEU. Thank you. Let me first thank Chairman Royce and
Ranking Member Engel for agreeing to have the next hearing be
on Russia. I think we all appreciate that. And thank you to the
panelists for being here, for your expertise and thank you, Dr.
Exum, for your military service.

As you know, Iran is involved in Syria, as is Russia, and there
are two news agencies, CNN and Reuters, reporting that the Pentagon is considering sending U.S. conventional ground forces to
Syria. That would significantly alter our military footprint and operations in Syria. I think it is a very, very bad idea.

The Trump administration has not laid out a plan for what they
would do there. They have not set out objectives they would want
them to achieve. The Trump administration has not explained who
they would support in Syria nor how long they would be there. I
would like to ask each of you, do any of you think it would be a
good idea to send our women and men of our military in harm's
way into Syria? And let me start with Dr. Exum.

Mr. EXUM. So, Congressman, you are asking all the right questions. If I could be so honest, I think that we would like to know
a lot more about what these soldiers would be doing. I think we
would want to know who they would be. I don't think, I mean you
followed this conflict closely. You know that our overall strategy
against the Islamic State has been by, with, and through local
partners. So we have had forces on the ground in Iraq and Syria
to the degree that they would enable local partners.

The strategic dilemma that this administration faces specifically
as it wants to go on Raqqa is whether or not you can push on
Raqqa without arming and training the YPG. Doing so would put
at risk our relationship with a NATO ally in Turkey, and I think
that is what this administration is wrestling with. We made the decision when we constructed the strategy to counter the Islamic
State which had buy-in from not only the civilians in the Pentagon
but also all the uniforms as well that working by, with, and
through local partners would make more sense, first off, because
many of us are Iraq veterans and we know that the Iraq war cost
roughly almost 5,000 U.S. lives.

I think during my tenure at the Department of Defense the way
in which we waged the conflict cost five, the loss of five U.S. serv-
icemen. It is also less expensive in terms of monetarily. But more
important than that strategically the logic is it is more sustainable
on the ground. Yes, it is messier. Yes, it takes more time. But if
local groups have a buy-in to the fight they have a buy-in to the
victory and that is something that didn't happen after we defeated
the insurgency in Iraq in 2007-2008.

To get back to your question, deviating from by, with, and through could potentially, you know, I would caution the administration from deploying the 82nd Airborne on the ground in northeastern Syria. I believe that would be a mistake. I believe it would be costly not just in terms of money but in terms of lives. If by contrast you are talking about limited conventional forces to help you breach the outer defenses of Raqqa in a way that might mean that you don't have to arm the YPG to the extent that would really inflame the relationship with Turkey, if that is what they are talking about that is something different.

So Congressman, I think you are asking all the right questions. If I am in the position of the Pentagon right now, I am really weighing those options and trying to think about, you know, which forces you are really talking about. So it all depends on kind of the forces that they are talking about.

Mr. LIEU. Thank you. So the other panelists, you don't have to answer unless you think it is a good idea to send a lot of ground troops into Syria. Do any of you think it is a good idea?

Mr. EXUM. No.

Mr. LIEU. All right. So I have limited time. I wanted to talk about Yemen, Doctor, as you have mentioned Yemen. As you know, Iran is involved there.

Mr. EXUM. That is right.

Mr. LIEU. I don't have any problem with freedom of navigation. What I have a problem with is the United States, we are refueling a Saudi-led coalition of aircraft that drop bombs in Yemen and we don't have any idea where they drop them. That has been told to us. I have gone to briefings, and we don't know.

And it turns out that there has been multiple airstrikes on civilians. Amnesty International and Human Rights Watch have documented over 70 unlawful airstrikes on wedding parties, on a Doctors Without Borders hospital, on schools; children, women, civilians are being slaughtered. These look like war crimes, and U.S. military should not be aiding and abetting war crimes. And what I want to know, Dr. Exum, is sort of your view on that issue.

Mr. EXUM. So Congressman, you put your finger on why I think the last administration was reluctant to get deeper involved in the conflict in Yemen. I think in some ways the last administration, to put it crudely, tried to be half pregnant. There is a strategic argument to be made for if you are going to get involved in the conflict then help the Saudis and the Emirates and their coalition win and help them win in a way that is compliant with the laws of armed conflict and that allows you to have some influence over the way they are involved, or you completely step away and you say that we can't be involved with this conflict.

I think we tried to find a middle ground and I think that is where that led to some of the confusion and some of the problems. I will say however that we do have adversaries in Yemen, al-Qaeda in the Arabian Peninsula, for example, the Islamic State in Yemen where it might make sense to partner with some of our forces on the ground, or some of our partners, the Emirates, for example, who are kind of a cut above the other Gulf forces in terms of their competence, and there it might make sense to partner with them.

Against threats to freedom of navigation that is something like I said, I think it is a U.S. interest. I also think it is a huge interest for the Europeans, for India, for South Korea, for anybody pushing shipping through the Bab al-Mandeb, and so there should be a concerted diplomatic effort to pressure the Iranians with respect to the presence of some anti-ship cruise missiles in Yemen, and if necessary there should also be a kinetic response, because that is a point where that has always been a key U.S. interest for 50 years in terms of freedom of navigation and commerce around the Arabian Peninsula, and I think you would want to take a hard stand there.

But I take your points regarding the broader conflict and I think it is one, it was a key topic of debate within the Obama administration, sir.

Chairman ROYCE. Well, thank you. Thank you. We want to thank again our panel. We appreciate the time of our witnesses today and especially, you know, this focus of what we do in the light of Iran's continued ballistic missile program and its continued transfer of missiles to Hezbollah and the other activities in the region that are threatening to the countries in the region. And as Ms. Bauer observed we should start, I think, with the premise that on these violations Iran gets no special pass.

And we look forward to continuing to work with each of you in terms of the challenges ahead, so thank you, and with that we stand adjourned.

[Whereupon, at 12:25 p.m., the committee was adjourned.]

APPENDIX

MATERIAL SUBMITTED FOR THE RECORD

FULL COMMITTEE HEARING NOTICE
COMMITTEE ON FOREIGN AFFAIRS
U.S. HOUSE OF REPRESENTATIVES
WASHINGTON, DC 20515-6128

Edward R. Royce (R-CA), Chairman

February 16, 2017

TO: MEMBERS OF THE COMMITTEE ON FOREIGN AFFAIRS

You are respectfully requested to attend an OPEN hearing of the Committee on Foreign Affairs, to be held in Room 2172 of the Rayburn House Office Building (and available live on the Committee website at http://www.ForeignAffairs.house.gov):

DATE: Thursday, February 16, 2017

TIME: 10:00 a.m.

SUBJECT: Iran on Notice

WITNESSES: Mr. Scott Modell
Managing Director
The Rapidan Group

Ms. Katherine Bauer
Blumenstein-Katz Family Fellow
The Washington Institute for Near East Policy

Mr. David Albright
Founder and President
Institute for Science and International Security

Andrew Exum, Ph.D.
Contributing Editor
The Atlantic

By Direction of the Chairman

COMMITTEE ON FOREIGN AFFAIRS
MINUTES OF FULL COMMITTEE HEARING

Day___*Thursday*___Date_____*2/16/2017*_____Room_____*2172*_____

Starting Time _____*10:10*_____ Ending Time _____*12:25*_____

Recesses |_*0*_| (____to____)(____to____)(____to____)(____to____)(____to____)(____to____)

Presiding Member(s)
Chairman Edward R. Royce, Rep. Joe Wilson

Check all of the following that apply:

Open Session ☑   Electronically Recorded (taped) ☑
Executive (closed) Session ☐   Stenographic Record ☑
Televised ☑

TITLE OF HEARING:
Iran on Notice

COMMITTEE MEMBERS PRESENT:
See attached.

NON-COMMITTEE MEMBERS PRESENT:
none

HEARING WITNESSES: Same as meeting notice attached? Yes ☑ No ☐
(If "no", please list below and include title, agency, department, or organization.)

STATEMENTS FOR THE RECORD: *(List any statements submitted for the record.)*
IFR - Rep. David Cicilline

TIME SCHEDULED TO RECONVENE _____
or
TIME ADJOURNED *12:25*

_____
Full Committee Hearing Coordinator

HOUSE COMMITTEE ON FOREIGN AFFAIRS

FULL COMMITTEE HEARING

PRESENT	MEMBER	PRESENT	MEMBER
X	Edward R. Royce, CA	X	Eliot L. Engel, NY
X	Christopher H. Smith, NJ	X	Brad Sherman, CA
X	Ileana Ros-Lehtinen, FL	X	Gregory W. Meeks, NY
X	Dana Rohrabacher, CA		Albio Sires, NJ
X	Steve Chabot, OH	X	Gerald E. Connolly, VA
X	Joe Wilson, SC	X	Theodore E. Deutch, FL
	Michael T. McCaul, TX		Karen Bass, CA
X	Ted Poe, TX	X	William Keating, MA
	Darrell Issa, CA	X	David Cicilline, RI
	Tom Marino, PA	X	Ami Bera, CA
	Jeff Duncan, SC		Lois Frankel, FL
	Mo Brooks, AL	X	Tulsi Gabbard, HI
X	Paul Cook, CA	X	Joaquin Castro, TX
X	Scott Perry, PA	X	Robin Kelly, IL
X	Ron DeSantis, FL		Brendan Boyle, PA
	Mark Meadows, NC	X	Dina Titus, NV
X	Ted Yoho, FL	X	Norma Torres, CA
X	Adam Kinzinger, IL	X	Brad Schneider, IL
X	Lee Zeldin, NY	X	Tom Suozzi, NY
X	Dan Donovan, NY	X	Adriano Espailat, NY
X	James F. Sensenbrenner, Jr., WI	X	Ted Lieu, CA
X	Ann Wagner, MO		
X	Brian J. Mast, FL		
X	Brian K. Fitzpatrick, PA		
X	Francis Rooney, FL		
X	Thomas A. Garrett, Jr., VA		

Congress of the United States
Washington, DC 20515

The Honorable Ed Royce
Committee on Foreign Affairs
2170 Rayburn House Office Building
Washington, DC 20515

February 14, 2017

Dear Chairman Royce:

We write to stress the urgent need for the House Committee on Foreign Affairs to investigate former National Security Advisor Michael Flynn's relationship with Russia, specifically whether he made promises to lift sanctions while he was a civilian after the 2016 election before President Trump took office. We believe General Flynn must appear before the Committee, under oath as soon as possible. General Flynn's resignation leaves many questions unanswered about his and President Trump's ties to Russia and whether American national security and intelligence operations have been compromised.

It has been widely reported that General Flynn spoke with Russian Ambassador to the United States Sergey Kislyak in late December shortly after the Obama Administration announced new sanctions on Russia due to its interference in the 2016 American presidential election. Since then, General Flynn has given conflicting answers as to whether he discussed those sanctions with Kislyak and whether he gave assurances to the Russian government that sanctions would be lifted under the Trump Administration. If he did so, he may have violated U.S. law. When American intelligence agencies and the Department of Justice learned of the details of Flynn's phone call, they warned the White House in late January that Flynn may be susceptible to blackmail. It does not appear that any action was taken by the White House to investigate this incident or review General Flynn's security clearance.

General Flynn's resignation yesterday leaves many important questions unanswered and the White House has indicated no willingness to address them. As stated in the House Foreign Affairs Committee Oversight Plan that was adopted on January 24, 2017, the Committee has jurisdiction over and will investigate "Kremlin-driven efforts to undermine the government, democratic and other institutions of the U.S. and other countries through cyber intrusions, propaganda and other tools." It continues, "The Committee will examine the range of options available to the U.S. to respond to these actions, including legislation to impose additional sanctions on Russia."

Our country's national security, independence, and democratic institutions are at stake. As the body within the House with jurisdiction over U.S. foreign policy, we would be negligent if we left the questions about this incident unanswered. We must investigate who from the Trump transition team was aware of contacts between General Flynn and Ambassador Kislyak, what was discussed, and what President Trump and Vice President Pence knew about this conversation and when they knew it.

The House Foreign Affairs Committee must use its authority to demand that General Flynn answer these questions, and shed light on his and the Trump Administration's relationship with the Russian government. The American people deserve these answers. We thank you for your attention to this matter.

Sincerely,

David N. Cicilline

Gregory Meeks

Gerald E. Connolly

Karen Bass

Ami Bera

Joaquin Castro

Brendan Boyle

Norma Torres

Adriano Espaillat

Bradley S. Schneider

Brad Sherman

Albio Sires

Theodore E. Deutch

William Keating

Lois Frankel

Robin Kelly

Dina Titus

Thomas Suozzi

Ted Lieu

Tulsi Gabbard